The Book of

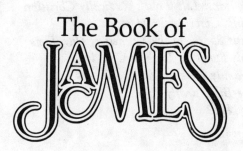

By the same author—

How to Study the Bible
Thessalonians: Life That's Radically Christian
Galatians: Gospel of Freedom
Colossians Speaks to the Sickness of Our Time
The Holy Spirit in Today's World
Is the Family Here to Stay?
Does the Bible Really Work?
What's New?

The Book of
JAMES

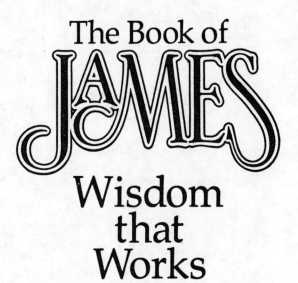

Wisdom
that
Works

David A. Hubbard

THETA
BOOKS

WORD BOOKS
PUBLISHER
4800 WEST WACO DRIVE
WACO. TEXAS
76703

All Scripture quotations are from The Revised Standard Version
of the Bible, copyright 1946, 1952, © 1971, 1973 by the Division of Christian Education of the National Council of the
Churches of Christ in the U.S.A., and used by permission.

ISBN 0-8499-2885-0
Library of Congress catalog card number: 79-63945
Printed in the United States of America

Contents

Introduction

Right from the beginning Christians have needed correcting. Though we may admire the zeal and courage of the first generation of believers, we should not idealize them. The New Testament itself rules that out. Virtually every one of its twenty-seven books was written to congregations or clusters of congregations whose faith or practice needed mending.

Heresies about the incarnation, doubts about Jesus' return, divisions based on strife and jealousy, abuse of spiritual gifts, intimidation at the hands of Rome, temptation to immorality and incest—these were the situations that called forth the holy books in the latter half of our Bible. No document gives clearer evidence of the need for correction that early Christians faced than the Book of James. It is a bundle of exhortations to clearer thinking, tougher patience, stronger love, more fervent prayer, and deeper trust.

Who wrote the book? The text itself gives little help to this question. "James, a servant of God and of the Lord Jesus Christ" is its cryptic answer. Of the men named James in the New Testament, only James, the brother of Jesus, is a suitable candidate, since John's brother James, son of Zebedee, died a martyr in the church's infancy (ca. A.D. 44—Acts 12:2). There is no indication that our Lord's brother (Matt. 13:55) accepted Jesus' authority during the days of his earthly ministry. The resurrection appearance noted by Paul must have been what convinced him of Jesus' lordship (1 Cor. 15:7) and also qualified him to be called an apostle (Gal. 1:19).

Indeed, he apparently served as the leader of the church at Jerusalem (Acts 12:17) until he was stoned to death on the orders of Ananus the high priest about A.D. 62. (Josephus, in his *Antiquities of the Jews* 20:197–203, described the circumstances in some detail.) James's prominence as a Christian leader who sought to maintain close ties with his Jewish faith is seen in the Jerusalem Council over which he presided (Acts 15) and his various encounters with Paul (Gal. 1:19, 2:9; Acts 21:18).

The absence of any mention of his blood-ties to Jesus or his apostleship may indicate both James's humility and the authority which his name alone carried among the early Christians, especially in Palestine and Syria. Much in the book accords with a date between A.D. 50 and 62, the heyday of James's ministry: (1) the organization of the churches is uncomplicated; (2) the commands to righteousness echo the themes and forms of Jesus' Sermon on the Mount (Matt. 5–7); (3) the absence of mention of Jesus' death and resurrection may indicate that these twin themes of the gospel were so well known to the Christians that no mention or interpretation of them was necessary. Though theories have been put forth that place the book later—at the end of the first century or beginning of the second—none of them has any more evidence to establish it than has the time-honored view that credits the work to the well-known James of Jerusalem.

Who were the original recipients? The simplest understanding of "the twelve tribes in the Dispersion" (1:1) to whom the book was addressed is that they are the entire church of Jesus Christ, God's new Israel, carrying out the mission of God's Messiah in the world. *Dispersion* here may indicate a geographical spread around the Mediterranean world, but even more it describes the pilgrim character of Christ's people, who sojourn on earth though their permanent abode is with God in heaven.

To what particular group of churches the letter was first sent we do not know. The absence of specifics— like names and places and evidence of personal acquaintance—has caused James to be placed in the New Testament beside the General (or Catholic) Epistles, whose authors are named but not their audiences. The broad phrase "twelve tribes" may suggest that the letter was intended for widespread circulation whenever believers encountered the persecution and the temptations described in the book.

If more specific suggestions about the recipients are desired, two possibilities may help. First, the letter may have been directed originally to the churches in Syria—at places like Antioch and Seleucia—that were key outposts of the Jerusalem church and represented the frontier where Jewish Christians mixed most readily with Gentiles. Second, the book may have been written at the request of Jewish Christians who had made pilgrimages to Jerusalem, heard James's teachings, and requested copies of them to take home with them to the far-flung cities of the Mediterranean. More definite than this, the evidence within the letter and outside does not allow us to be.[1]

What kind of book is it? Though we may call James's work a *letter*, it takes a bit of license to do so. It has, of course, the formal beginning of a letter (author, recipients, and greetings), but it lacks, as we noted, personal characteristics, such as the mention of names, relationships, and specific problems. Furthermore, it ends abruptly, without valediction or benediction.

The Book of James comes closer to being a *sermon* or *lecture* than a letter. It is a cluster of exhortations that order Christian conduct, with imperatives dominating the grammar. Much of the illustrative material is drawn from the Old Testament (references to Abraham—2:21–24; Rahab—2:25; Job—5:11; and Elijah—5:17–18), and a lot of the subject matter is drawn from Hebrew wisdom literature: patience in suffering (1:2–4, 12–15, 5:11), dependence on God for wisdom (1:5–8), control of tongue and temper (1:19–21, 26, 3:1–12), demonstration of righteousness in practical living (1:22–27, 2:1–26), centrality of wisdom as a way of life (3:13), contrast between wise and foolish conduct (3:15–17), submission to God's sovereign

---

[1] For these and other suggestions about the authorship and background of James, see R. P. Martin, *New Testament Foundations,* vol. 2 (Grand Rapids, MI: Eerdmans, 1978), pp. 358–65.

will in the making of plans (4:13–17), concern for
justice toward the poor and equity in business practices
(5:1–6), desire to save others from error (5:19–20).
All of these themes remind us of familiar passages
in Job, Proverbs, and Ecclesiastes.

These wisdom subjects are matched by the use of
literary forms common to Israel's sages: exhortations
followed by the motive for the exhortation (1:2–3,
19–20); use of analogies and figures of speech for
clarity (looking into a mirror—1:23; bits, rudders, and
fire as illustrations of the tongue—3:3–5); rhetorical questions (3:11–12); quotations of proverbs (4:6
from Prov. 3:34); addresses to audiences probably
not present (called technically *apostrophe*—4:13–16,
5:1–6); illustrations from everyday life (the farmer's
patience—5:7). Along with Jesus' Sermon on the
Mount, with which they have much in common,
James's teaching techniques give us a window on how
the early church was instructed in the ramifications
of the gospel as it was applied to every area of life.

What is the purpose of the book? Instruction of believers
in the demands of Christian discipleship is the short
answer to this question. The exact situation which
called for such instruction is hard to pinpoint.

The strong words of discipline uttered by James
suggest one factor in the circumstances of his readers:
they may have been tempted to take advantage of
their Christian liberty and ease away from their responsibilities to practice godliness and compassion.
Paul's teachings on faith as the means by which we
appropriate God's salvation had been cheapened by

some who confused faith in God (which means whole-hearted commitment, total loyalty, full dependence) with belief about God. It was this perversion of the gospel that provoked James's warnings about hearing without doing and believing without loving. His answer to these primitive—and ever-present—distortions was not the return to legalism but the response of love, the freedom of the law of liberty (1:25).

The need for patience in persecution seems to be another dominant strand woven through the book. One recent suggestion by my colleague Ralph P. Martin may be helpful. He has called attention to the tensions in James's day between the wealthy aristocracy, including the leaders of the Temple, and the poorer priests and commoners. The haughty, often oppressive decisions of the upper classes, especially the Sadducees, provoked rash and revolutionary activity from a party called the Zealots. Was this tension between Zealot and aristocrat part of the "wars" and "fightings among you" that James decried (4:1)? James's position in this conflict seems to have been a delicate one. On the one hand, he had to protest the oppressions and exploitation of the peasant classes; on the other he had to warn the oppressed against the ruthless and ultimately profitless bloodshed that the Zealots engaged in.

These two notes—resistance against economic and social abuse, yet patience to allow God to do the judging—helped to shape the message of James to the churches. They may also have been what cost him his life. Dr. Martin finds a hint of James's martyrdom in 5:6: "You have condemned, you have killed the righteous man; he does not resist you." One of James's traditional titles was *the Just* (or *Righteous;* the Greek word can be translated either way). It may be that the final editor of the work, who is also responsible for the excellent Greek style, included that reference to his executed teacher.[2]

The world where most of us live today as sons and daughters of the "twelve tribes in the Dispersion" may not seem riddled with animosities as sharp as those faced by James and his flock. But the need for wisdom is no less. There are a thousand ways in which our spirits can go sour, our minds turn doubtful, our hearts boil with vindictiveness, our tongues ooze venom. Wisdom to catch the gospel's call to loving service, wisdom to wait for the Savior's return and the true justice that it will bring, and wisdom to work for that justice with its shelter to widows and orphans, foreigners and laborers, is every bit as needful as it was when God's Spirit prodded James to lay down for his people his winsome wisdom—his wisdom that works.

---

[2] R. P. Martin, in *Biblical and Near Eastern Studies,* ed. G. A. Tuttle (Grand Rapids, MI: Eerdmans, 1978), pp. 97–103.

1.

Wisdom to Stand Life's Tests

James 1:1-8

James, a servant of God and of the Lord Jesus Christ,
To the twelve tribes in the Dispersion:
Greeting.
Count it all joy, my brethren, when you meet various
trials, for you know that the testing of your faith produces
steadfastness. And let steadfastness have its full effect, that
you may be perfect and complete, lacking in nothing.
If any of you lacks wisdom, let him ask God, who gives
to all men generously and without reproaching, and it will
be given him. But let him ask in faith, with no doubting,
for he who doubts is like a wave of the sea that is driven
and tossed by the wind. For that person must not suppose
that a double-minded man, unstable in all his ways, will
receive anything from the Lord.

For Christians, testings come in many shapes and
sizes. It has been so from the beginning. Both Jews

and Gentiles in the early church felt the sting of opposition.

When Jewish Christians confessed Jesus as the Messiah, they were frequently cut off from the warmth of their families and the shelter of their synagogues. Friends shunned them, employers fired them, officials harassed them. Their faith was put to stringent tests almost before it had opportunity to take root.

For Gentile believers the situation was much the same. Their relatives and neighbors cherished their pagan superstitions and built their lives around them. Civil and religious life were tightly tied together. Festivals and holidays were geared to give expression to pagan practices. To refuse to participate meant that Christians were moving against the crowd with the kind of strange loneliness that we feel if we try to drive the wrong direction down a crowded one-way street. The Gentiles who became Christians faced another major problem: they lived in cultures where religion and immorality went hand in hand. Their loyalty to Christ and the discipline of their new faith were tried sorely as they watched the sensual revelings of their kinsmen. The war of Spirit with flesh for them was painful combat.

During two fierce periods in the first century of our Christian era, the pressure on believers in the Roman world became almost unbearable. The intensity was due to savage persecution implemented by two emperors and their armies: Nero (A.D. 54–68) and Domitian (A.D. 81–96). It was Nero who blamed the great Roman fire of A.D. 64 on Christians, sparking a huge blaze of resentment against them which resulted in torture and death for many. Both of the pillar apostles, Paul and Peter, were put to death at his behest.

Thirty years later, Domitian repeated this pattern of persecution with a vehemence that outdid Nero. Under Domitian John was exiled to Patmos, the Mediterranean island where he wrote the Book of Revelation. Frustrated by the failure of his military campaigns, Domitian sought to assure his prestige by declaring himself *Dominus et Deus,* Lord and God. The refusal of Christians and Jews to acknowledge that claim led to their violent persecution. Domitian's ruthlessness became so savage that even the pagan population of the empire protested, and the brutal emperor was finally assassinated.

These vicious assaults on God's people are part of our Christian history. They happened to people who by ties of faith and Spirit are linked to us. Some of the books of the New Testament were written specifically to help believers endure the pressures that were being brought against their faith. 1 Peter (from Nero's day), and Revelation (from Domitian's era), are two such writings.

The letter of James, too, is of special interest because it is a treasury of advice to beleaguered Christians, designed to give them wisdom for living full and joyful lives under harsh circumstances. "Wisdom from above" is its theme. It points us to the vast resources that God has to steady and strengthen his people in difficult times.

It was probably not Nero's shadow or Domitian's that hovered over the parchment of James as the Holy Spirit moved him to write, though we cannot be sure. But certainly bleak trial was the context. Christians were being pressed by persecution more economic and social than political. The problems were urgent, and the needs were great. The rich and privileged were oppressing the poor commoners. Two great temptations faced the struggling Christian: the temptation to despair and the temptation to revolt. Neither was God's way. Nothing less than wisdom from above—wisdom to stand life's tests—would see them through.

James told us almost nothing about himself—except the most important thing: he was a servant of God and of the Lord Jesus Christ. The word *servant* is key: (1) it speaks of James's obedience to God as one of his ministers; (2) it marks James as a worshiper of God and of the Lord Jesus; (3) it linked him with the wise and righteous Servant of the Lord through whom Israel was ministered to in Isaiah's prophecies (Isa. 42, 53) and, consequently, underlined his authority to speak on God's behalf.

His audience was especially vulnerable to persecution because it was scattered: "To the twelve tribes in the Dispersion" he sent his greetings (1:1). The Dispersion was the official term used to describe Jews who had moved or been driven from the homeland in Palestine and had taken up residence throughout the Greco-Roman world. Egypt, North Africa, Babylon, Syria, Arabia, Asia Minor, Greece, Italy—even

Spain—all had become ports of refuge for Jews on the move. Living in scattered colonies, clinging together in their synagogues, many of them became ready converts to the Christian faith as the Church moved out on its mission after Pentecost.

Gentile converts frequently joined them, and together these little bands of believers sought to glorify God in a hostile world. These "twelve tribes," as James called them, were the people of God, the new Israel—Jew and Gentile together. They refused to participate in pagan ceremonies; they refused to acknowledge any emperor as Lord and God, because that honor already belonged to Jesus the Christ whom they loved and served.

Joy Based on Steadfastness

James lost no time in getting to his main theme. No personal remarks, no individual greetings, no general comments distracted from his goal. The situation was too serious for that: "Count it all joy, my brethren, when you meet various trials, for you know that the testing of your faith produces steadfastness" (1:2-3).

Joy and trial seem incompatible terms. Indeed, if joy were our aim, trial might be the last place we would look for it—just as the refrigerator would be the last place we would check to see how the roast is cooking.

Yet joy is the attitude that James advocated. Indeed, *all* joy, extreme joy, full joy, is what he counseled.

Why? Certainly not for any sick reasons, as though

we were masochists, eager for pain to increase our pleasure. And not for any deceptive reasons, as though he were telling us that persecution was not really painful, or that if we smiled it would go away.

We should rejoice in trials because *joy will help us endure them.* Consider the alternatives. Despair? It saps our energies, weakens our resistance, and makes us more vulnerable both to the pain that persecution inflicts and to the unbelief which is persecution's aim. Anger? Of course, unjust suffering inflicted by ruthless people can make our blood boil, but if we cannot control our anger we are prone to become violent ourselves and contribute to the evil cause, and not to Christ's kingdom. Bitterness? That may be the worst response of all, because it tends to make God the enemy. Why did he get me into this mess? Why hasn't he gotten me out of it? The persecution has no meaning, and God seems only to let things get worse. That will be our conclusion, if we let bitterness take root.

Joy, in contrast, will help us to keep our composure, to be as positive as possible, and to make the most of a bad situation. "Count it all joy, brethren, when you meet various trials."

We should rejoice in trials, because *trials cannot do us ultimate hurt.* Remember James's words: "For you know that the testing of your faith produces steadfastness." What is being tested by our suffering? Our intelligence? No, pain can muddle our thinking. Our will power? No, brutality or violence, as in the brainwashing endured by prisoners of war, may weaken our wills and make it hard for us to tell right from wrong. But what is being tested? Our faith.

Reflect a moment on what faith is. It is our confidence in God, our loyalty to him, for what he has done for us in sending Jesus to die for our sins and rise again to conquer death. Faith is our response to what God has done in the past and will do in the future. What can persecution change? Can it undo Christ's death so as to make us unforgiven? Can it reverse the victory of the resurrection so that death once more becomes the winner? Can it cancel the second coming so that we are robbed of all hope? Of course not! is the answer I hear pounding back.

Persecution cannot undermine what God has done. But what about our response? That is part of faith, too. But wait a minute. Does my faith depend only on me? Was it not the Word of God that helped me believe? Was it not the Spirit of God who both called me and helped me say "yes"? Then is faith not a gift that God has given? If so, how can trials take it away? Joy is possible because the ultimate hurt—the loss of our faith in God—is not the necessary result no matter what else, in goods or blood, persecution may cost us.

We should rejoice in trials, because *trials will work beneficial results*. Steadfastness is what suffering can lead to. Opposition and misunderstanding are like heat that will make metal harder. Manufacturers always put steel tools through heat-treating—a process designed to harden the layers of molecules close to the surface so that the metal will not chafe or crumble when the hammer pounds or the pliers grip.

God's interest in our characters leads him to use heat to toughen our resistance. Refinement, maturity, growth are what he aims for us. And what an aim that is! Worth taking heat for! A great basis for rejoicing!

Small wonder that James can exhort his scattered friends to "let steadfastness have its full effect, that you may be perfect and complete, lacking in nothing" (1:4).

Wisdom Rooted in Faith

If joy is one gift that we need to cope with suffering, wisdom is the other: "If any of you lacks wisdom, let him ask God, who gives to all men generously and without reproaching, and it will be given him" (1:5).

Times of trial put human wisdom to the test. Think of the questions posed. *Why?* What lies behind this suffering? Is it judgment that I deserve? Is it a witness to the unbelieving world who need to learn lessons of trust? Is it discipline to encourage my growth and maturation? Why? Only wisdom can come close to answering that.

What? is the other question that trials put to us. What should I do to cope with them? What should I do to help others who are in the same plight? What can I do to get the suffering to stop? Only wisdom can help with such puzzles.

And *such wisdom God has offered in full generosity.* God can be generous with his wisdom; he has an unlimited supply of it. God's wisdom is not a fossil-fuel millennium in the making but now running short. He is the God of all wisdom.

He does not begrudge giving wisdom to us who ask, because wisdom is not something that anyone can have too much of. *Too smart* for his own good, we sometimes say. *Too smart* is our phrase; not *too wise.* Wisdom by definition means the ability to use well what we have. God can lavish on us all that we need, because the wisdom he gives equips us to use it well.

Such wisdom God has offered in response to our faith: "But let him ask in faith, with no doubting, for he who doubts is like a wave of the sea that is driven and tossed by the wind. For that person must not suppose that a double-minded man, unstable in all his ways, will receive anything from the Lord" (1:6–8).

Faith is required for obvious reasons. Unless we truly trust God we are not sure whether we need his help. Suffering tends to make us scattered in our thoughts. We are tempted to try one route, then another, for escape. The wind-tossed wave is a good example. It is impossible to chart a course by it, let alone build a house on it. Until we are so desperate for God's help that we trust him alone, we are not really serious about our needs. Whenever we think we can solve our own major problems, we have not yet learned what great trouble we are really in.

Faith is necessary for another reason. If we do not truly trust God, we may not use the wisdom he gives. Half-hearted trust in a doctor usually results in half-hearted (or half-witted) following of his orders. Faith is essential to obedience. Only when we fully trust the God of wisdom will we use well the wisdom he gives.

Joy based on steadfastness and wisdom rooted in faith—what twin gifts of life and love to an abused people. Joy gives us the outlook we need to see our way through. Wisdom gives us the insight we need to work our way through.

Suffering and persecution, trials that test our faith, come in all shapes and sizes. But God's joy, based on the joy that Jesus took with him to the cross, is ready to fit whatever shape our suffering takes. And God's wisdom, expressed in the ability the Holy Spirit gives us to make sound decisions even under pressure, will stretch to any size.

Suffering will always be part of our earthly lot as God's faithful. Joy and wisdom will always be part of God's heavenly provision. We can count on the one as surely as the other.

2.

Wisdom to Face Life's Realities

James 1:9-18

Let the lowly brother boast in his exaltation, and the rich in his humiliation, because like the flower of the grass he will pass away. For the sun rises with its scorching heat and withers the grass; its flower falls, and its beauty perishes. So will the rich man fade away in the midst of his pursuits.

Blessed is the man who endures trial, for when he has stood the test he will receive the crown of life which God has promised to those who love him. Let no one say when he is tempted, "I am tempted by God"; for God cannot be tempted with evil and he himself tempts no one; but each person is tempted when he is lured and enticed by his own desire. Then desire when it has conceived gives birth to sin; and sin when it is full-grown brings forth death.

Do not be deceived, my beloved brethren. Every good endowment and every perfect gift is from above, coming down from the Father of lights with whom there is no variation or shadow due to change. Of his own will he brought us forth by the word of truth that we should be a kind of first fruits of his creatures.

Facing reality is not easy. When we think about it, this is surprising, because some areas of reality we do handle rather well. Most of us can count accurately the number of eggs in the refrigerator; we can measure correctly the amount of yardage needed for the new drapes; we can balance our bank statements within a few dollars—or even a few pennies. All of these tasks of measuring and counting are exercises in dealing with reality. We do them rather well—just as we figure our income taxes with reasonable correctness and follow a complicated recipe with sufficient control to win the family's praise for the tasty casserole.

Despite our successes in these areas, the original statement holds: facing reality is not easy. What makes the difference? Why can we deal with many realities—from the length of our drapes to the size of our tax bill—with firm objectivity, yet find ourselves running from other obvious facts of life? Why can we see some issues just as they are, the number of eggs in a tray for instance, while other issues are either brightened or darkened by the fantasies with which we color them?

The basic difference, I suppose, is how threatening or how attractive the reality is. Two barking dogs that stalk us on a dark night will seem like a pack of hungry wolves. Under threat, we magnify reality and make it larger than life. When we are exhausted from fatigue or despair, every molehill looms like a mountain; every pothole in our path yawns like the Grand Canyon. Our inadequacy distorts our view of reality so that we cannot face it for what it is.

Attraction as well as threat pushes our perspective out of shape. To an uncoordinated teenager the decathlon champion must look like a Greek god, capable of all wonders and immune to all suffering. To an adolescent fighting problems of acne and overweight, the perfect skin and lithe frame of the magazine model must seem like utopia itself. It would be hard for the young person who struggles with his or her own sense of worth to believe that the model has any problems at all. How could any creature so glamorous have any frustrations with family, any battle with insecurity, any feelings of inadequacy?

Facing reality takes special wisdom, wisdom to admit our inability to see things as they really are, wisdom to correct the distortions that plague us, wisdom to accept the lot that God has given us and to take responsibility for our conduct.

It was this kind of wisdom that James offered to his hearers—the poor Christians scattered along the Mediterranean coast. The opposition of the Roman leadership, the hostility of the pagan neighbors, and the oppression of Jewish aristocrats made wisdom all the more necessary. Persecution has its own way of fogging our perspective. It may make us envy those whose circumstances shield them from the pain afflicting us, and it may make us blame God for the evil we do in the midst of our suffering. Envy and blame were the twin attitudes that James's friends seem to have developed in the midst of their woes. Both attitudes stemmed from a failure to face life's realities.

The Reality That Wealth Is Only Transitory

"Let the lowly brother boast in his exaltation, and the rich in his humiliation, because like the flower of the grass he will pass away. For the sun rises with its scorching heat and withers the grass; its flower falls, and its beauty perishes. So will the rich man fade away in the midst of his pursuits" (1:9–11). It does not take much reading between the lines to hear these words as a warning against envy. Apparently these young Christians lived in societies where many of their neighbors had accumulated wealth. The cities around the Mediterranean were great mercantile centers, bustling with commercial activity. The power and freedom that such wealth could purchase had gone to the heads of the wealthy. Throughout his letter, James listed symptoms of this pride: (1) cruel oppression that hauled Christians into court, probably on trumped-up charges (2:6); (2) blasphemy of the very name of Christ by which Christians were called at their baptism (2:7); (3) boasting in their plans for trade and travel, as though they were lords of their own lives (4:13–17); (4) fraud and greed in cheating their laborers of the wages rightly due them (5:1–6).

Yet these were the persons that the Christians seemed to envy. Why? Persecution had apparently blinded them to the true realities of life—including the reality that wealth is only transitory. Their dimness of vision made them kin to one of the psalmists:

> But as for me, my feet had almost stumbled,
>   my steps had well nigh slipped.
> For I was envious of the arrogant,
>   when I saw the prosperity of the wicked.
>
> For they have no pangs;
>   their bodies are sound and sleek.
> They are not in trouble as other men are;
>   they are not stricken like other men.
> Therefore pride is their necklace;
>   violence covers them as a garment.
>
> *Psalm 73:2–6*

We can only guess at the reason for the envy: the ability of the wealthy to avoid the persecution and the hardships that the believers struggled with. The power, prominence and prestige that the rich enjoyed apparently shielded them from the possibility of any oppression. Indeed, some of them may have been among the oppressors.

James hit this misguided envy head-on: (1)*Those who depend on human wealth for security will wilt and die like a flower* in the blazing Mediterranean sun or the blasting desert wind. Our Old Testament psalmist had learned this lesson when he went to the sanctuary and discovered how God dealt with those—no matter how wealthy and powerful—who were not loyal to him:

> Truly thou dost set them in slippery places;
>   thou dost make them fall to ruin.

How they are destroyed in a moment,
swept away utterly by terrors!

Psalm 73:18–19

Who can envy a tumbling shack or a shriveling tuft
of grass? (2) *Those who depend on God*—no matter how
poor—*are the ones who will be exalted.* The only glory
available to the wealthy is that they may be humiliated
and thus learn to trust the Lord.

The poor will go up; the rich must go down. This
reversal of lots and stations should come as no surprise
to those who know the gospel. From the beginning,
the Virgin Mary perceived what God would do in
the new age which her Messiah was to bring:

"And his mercy is on those who fear him
from generation to generation.

. . . .

he has put down the mighty from their thrones,
and exalted those of low degree;
he has filled the hungry with good things,
and the rich he has sent empty away."

Luke 1:50, 52–53

Pity, not envy, is the realistic attitude that we should
have toward the affluent who have not yet been hum-
bled by the grace of God.

The Reality That Temptation Is Our Responsibility

Suffering carries with it special temptations. Depending on our personal make-up and the circum-

stances in which we find ourselves, we are tempted to turn bitter or vindictive. Doubt, anger, compromise—these and a host of other possibilities bubble up within us when the temperatures of life begin to heat. Keeping our eyes on reality is no simple matter when emotions start to boil.

One of the worst things that we can do in such times is to blame God for our attitudes. Apparently some of James's suffering friends had fallen into this trap: "Blessed is the man who endures trial, for when he has stood the test he will receive the crown of life which God has promised to those who love him. Let no one say when he is tempted, 'I am tempted by God'; for God cannot be tempted with evil and he himself tempts no one; but each person is tempted when he is lured and enticed by his own desire" (James 1:12–14).

Face reality, James was saying—the reality that temptation is *our* responsibility. He gave his hearers positive encouragement to do this, in *his reminder that true happiness comes to those who endure temptation.* They are the ones whom God honors, and to be honored by him is an ultimate definition of happiness.

James followed this reminder with *his instruction that God is neither susceptible to temptation himself nor inclined to inflict it on others.* Here the line is delicate. God is in charge of the outward circumstances of our lives. As in the Book of Job, he sets the limits to Satan's activity; no outward harm can come to us that God does not allow. We trust him for the shape and tone of our circumstances. We trust him so much, James

has already told us, that "we count it all joy" when
the trials come, while we ask God for wisdom to endure the trials and to learn from them.

The outward circumstances are God's concern; our
response to them is our responsibility. If wicked attitudes or foolish deeds are our answer to life's testings,
we can only blame ourselves. God does not give those
kinds of answers.

To blame God for our failure is not only unrealistic,
it is destructive. If we do not see where we are wrong,
how do we ask his forgiveness and seek his help?
Blaming God for our faults is a dead-end street; it
leads us nowhere.

James continued his look at reality with *his warning
that this temptation to blame God for our weaknesses must
be nipped in the bud.* The illustration that he used follows
a cycle of life from seduction to conception to birth
to full growth. One stage leads inevitably to the next:
temptation begins with our desires that seduce us;
desire given into results in sin; sin has no destiny
but death. His point is clear: deal with temptation
at the first stage—desire—and avoid the string of consequences that will follow if you do not deal with
it.

James's last word comes back to the person of God.
It is *his affirmation that God's purposes for us are not to
trap us with temptation but to bless us with good gifts:*
"Do not be deceived, my beloved brethren. Every
good endowment and every perfect gift is from above,
coming down from the Father of lights with whom
there is no variation or shadow due to change" (1:16–

17). Is God a fiendish tempter who puts us in tight places, waiting for us to fail so that he can pounce on us in judgment? Of course not; he is a good Giver whose unchanging disposition of love and faithfulness we can count on. More steady than the planets, which move and fade in response to his orders as their Creator, is his concern for the well-being of his people.

He has no will to heckle us, harass us, or mock us. His will is that our reverent and obedient lives will be models of goodness for the whole creation: "Of his own will he brought us forth by the word of truth that we should be a kind of first fruits of his creatures" (1:18). As a mother delivers a fresh, new life, so God has brought us to birth. And his plan is that we should bring the same kind of hope and cheer to the world that the early harvest of any crop brings to the farmer and his customers.

There is no room for envying the rich, no room for blaming God in this picture. God has called his people to better, higher, things: joy, not blame, in trials; gratitude, not greed, in the face of poverty and oppression.

And best of all, as the unchanging Giver of good gifts, he has offered us wisdom to make us grateful and joyous. If persecution and tribulation are part of everyday reality for many Christians, so are the wisdom and bounty of our God. It is his reality, more than anything else, that we want to face.

3.

Wisdom to Determine Life's Priorities

James 1:19-27

Know this, my beloved brethren. Let every man be quick to hear, slow to speak, slow to anger, for the anger of man does not work the righteousness of God. Therefore put away all filthiness and rank growth of wickedness and receive with meekness the implanted word, which is able to save your souls.

But be doers of the word, and not hearers only, deceiving yourselves. For if any one is a hearer of the word and not a doer, he is like a man who observes his natural face in a mirror; for he observes himself and goes away and at once forgets what he was like. But he who looks into the perfect law, the law of liberty, and perseveres, being no hearer that forgets but a doer that acts, he shall be blessed in his doing.

If any one thinks he is religious, and does not bridle his tongue but deceives his heart, this man's religion is vain. Religion that is pure and undefiled before God and the Father is this: to visit orphans and widows in their affliction, and to keep oneself unstained from the world.

Our national magazines—*Time* and *Newsweek,* for instance—lead us astray quite regularly. It is not inaccuracies in reporting the news that prompts that statement. By and large, the major magazines are no more or less reliable in their accounts of what is happening than the wire services, metropolitan newspapers, or television reports.

Their inaccuracies or prejudices may wrinkle our foreheads occasionally, especially when we personally know the details of a story. But it would be unfair to list them as the means of misleading us.

The basic error that these magazines commit—and we should not underestimate the potential damage—is to treat religion as one of life's departments. You know the usual format: Leaf past the early ads and letters to the editor, and you find that political news of the United States or Canada will lead the way. Press on and you will come to the brief survey of world events—a quick glimpse of what has gone on in Europe, South America, Asia, and Africa. Pause for a moment as you turn the pages and you can read a few terse words about famous persons, usually highlighted with photos. Persevere in your browsing and you will discover sections on law, art, literature, cinema, sports, business—and religion.

A department, perhaps more, a compartment of life—that is how the news magazines treat religion. Nothing could be more deceptive in its emphasis; nothing could be more wrong in its priorities. With all the wisdom they may have in tracking down stories, tracing trends, and checking their sources for consistency, the editors of the great magazines are lacking in wisdom. They do not know that religion is not a department of life; it is the whole affair. It is not a pigeonhole into which some of our spiritual activities are crammed; it is a canopy which casts its shadow over all we do.

We are many things—we complex and perplexed sons and daughters of Adam and Eve. We do live political lives in which our governments are a dominant reality. We are part of a shrinking globe where the major events in any country are news everywhere else. We are an empathetic race who laugh at and cry over the follies and the failings of our fellow human beings. And we are interested in and influenced by the trends in art, business, law, theater, literature—and a host of other fields.

In all these pursuits and endeavors, our religious beliefs determine what we value and how we respond. It takes priority—not just as the most important topic but as the lens through which we look at everything else. What is politics but one of the means by which we seek to express our biblical concerns for love and justice in a broken world? What is literature but a method of expressing human emotions and human needs? What is law but a way of protecting us from the ravages of human sin?

Our perspective on religion takes priority because it governs—or should govern—the rest of our thinking and living. But even then we have a problem. How does our religious faith, our spiritual commitment, express itself? What are the most consistent, the most mature, the most effective ways for us to bear witness to what we believe?

The friends of James in Syria and beyond puzzled over these questions. Indeed, some of them may not have puzzled enough. Amid the hardships of opposition and persecution, they were sorely tempted to express their faith in understandable, yet unacceptable, ways: (1) when trials came, they were tempted to discouragement, until God's wisdom taught them to receive adversity with joy (1:2–8); (2) when they gave in to temptations to doubt or anger, they wanted to blame God, until he gave them the wisdom to face their own responsibility (1:9–18); (3) when opposition heated, they expressed their religious commitment by bitterly berating their enemies, until God gave them wisdom to listen with meekness and to love with meaning (1:19–27).

Listening with Meekness

"Know this, my beloved brethren. Let every man be quick to hear, slow to speak, slow to anger, for the anger of man does not work the righteousness of God. Therefore put away all filthiness and rank growth of wickedness and receive with meekness the implanted word, which is able to save your souls" (1:19–21).

Once again we have to try to discover the situation James was addressing on the basis of his brief exhortations. Christians who spoke, perhaps preached, in anger seem to have been the problem. Their suffering had distorted their views of God's Word and fired their tongues with words of wrath.

Perhaps they were trying to get even with their oppressors by heaping words of revenge upon them. The Old Testament contains such pronouncements and prayers by the dozen, especially in the Psalms. Wracked by bitterness, enraged by pain, the Christians may have been taking words like the Jews uttered against their Babylonian captors and clubbing their enemies with them: "Happy shall he be who takes your little ones and dashes them against the rock!" (Ps. 137:9).

That *anger is not the way to work God's righteousness* was part of James' rebuke. Harsh, vindictive speech— even though supposedly based on God's Word—is not the way to accomplish God's justice. What does our anger do but snatch the judge's gavel from God's hands and rip the judge's gown from his shoulders? Anger makes us the judge. We do the condemning, the damning. We forget that vengeance is God's responsibility, and his alone.

That *meekness is the way to receive God's salvation* was the other part of James's warning. Doubtless there echoed in his ears the words of Jesus, quoted in part from Psalm 37:22, 29: "Blessed are the meek, for they shall inherit the earth" (Matt. 5:5). How out of joint that beatitude seemed. All around them, Christians were being driven from their homes and their lands by ruthless oppressors. It was the vicious who were gaining the inheritance, not the meek. Yet meekness was the solution James offered to the filth and wickedness of anger: "Receive with meekness the implanted word, which is able to save your souls."

What is meekness? It is not timidity, shyness, or cowardice. It is strength under control; it is power that is so subject to discipline that it will be used only for helpful purposes; it is restraint from violent action coupled with dependence on God, who alone can set life right.

As James uses the term here, *meekness* is wisdom to let God teach us life's priorities. He does that through "the implanted word." The language suggests *growth:* change may not take place all at once; it takes a while for seed, even the seed of the Word, to germinate and to bear its fruit. The language also suggests *assimilation:* the implanted word, rooted in our hearts by God's Spirit, becomes part of the fiber of our being. It is not law imposed from without; it is discipline fostered from within.

Loving with Meaning

The implanted word is an inward reminder of the nature of love: (1) it tells us how God loved us when we were his enemies; (2) it informs us that Jesus took abuse without reviling his attackers; (3) it urges us to love our enemies and to do good to those who use us badly; (4) it describes the character of a love that believes all things, bears all things, and hopes for all things.

As we listen with meekness, "quick to hear, slow to speak," the Holy Spirit who first inspired the Word exhorts and instructs us in the meaning of love and in loving with meaning. The implanted word which James mentioned and the spiritual fruit which Paul described (Gal. 5:22 ff.) bring the same result—a life so changed that love, not hatred, is its style. And this change demonstrates that the implanted word, meekly received, has saved us.

To love with meaning involves *doing the word as well as hearing it:* "But be doers of the word, and not hearers only, deceiving yourselves. For if any one is a hearer of the word and not a doer, he is like a man who observes his natural face in a mirror; for he observes himself and goes away and at once forgets what he was like. But he who looks into the perfect law, the law of liberty, and perseveres, being no hearer that forgets but a doer that acts, he shall be blessed in his doing" (James 1:22–25).

A quick look, a hurried hearing, is not enough. The Word of God is a mirror into which we are to peer patiently, seeking to see our needs and God's provision for them. Growth and discernment take time. No one learns to be a good lover in haste.

"The perfect law, the law of liberty" are James's descriptions of the biblical theme of love—the new commandment that Jesus taught and modeled: "A new commandment I give to you, that you love one another; even as I have loved you, that you also love one another. By this all men will know that you are my disciples, if you have love for one another" (John 13:34–35). This love had to embrace even the ruthless rich that made life so miserable for the Christians.

Jesus laid down just that kind of law: "For if you love [only] those who love you, what reward have you? Do not even the tax collectors do the same? . . . You, therefore, must be perfect, as your heavenly Father is perfect" (Matt. 5:46, 48).

The perfect law is the law that best follows God's perfect example in his love even for those who do not love him. And this perfect law is also a law of liberty—not a law that constricts, but a law that sets us free. Anger and hatred are not freedom. They tie us in knots; they goad us to say and do things that we do not really believe in. Love is liberating because it trusts God to be the final judge and encourages us to do good wherever we can.

In the struggle for priorities, then, listening to God's Word and loving on his terms come first. They define what it means to be religious and how true religious faith has to color everything else we do.

To love with meaning requires *helping those who cannot help themselves:* "If any one thinks he is religious, and does not bridle his tongue but deceives his heart, this man's religion is vain. Religion that is pure and undefiled before God and the Father is this: to visit orphans and widows in their affliction, and to keep oneself unstained from the world" (James 1:26–27). Here James has come full circle; he has returned to the problem with which he began: how do we show our religious faith in a hostile environment?

His answer is clear: we do not berate our enemies as though we were judges, "for the anger of man does not work the righteousness of God" (1:20). What *does* work the righteousness, what *is* a clear sign that we want justice to be done, is our care of the helpless—the widows and orphans. If ordinary Christians were afflicted by the meanness and selfishness of their wealthy and powerful neighbors, how much more were the widows and orphans who had no families to protect them? God's people had to put meaning into their love by caring for them in the name of him whom the psalmist called "Father of the fatherless and protector of widows" (Ps. 68:5).

Anger, hostility, vindictiveness are the world's way. There the helpless are abused and exploited. True religion—religion based on a commitment to the saving power of the God and Father of Jesus Christ—shuns those worldly ways as though they were an unbleachable stain.

The implanted word, not the national news magazines, is what we depend on to teach us how crucial true religion is. That word, as we hear it and do it, shows us that love, not anger, is the true law of life. It also shows us that the cross of forgiveness, not the gavel of judgment, is the finest symbol of faith.

4.

Wisdom to Treat People Right

James 2:1-7

My brethren, show no partiality as you hold the faith of our Lord Jesus Christ, the Lord of glory. For if a man with gold rings and in fine clothing comes into your assembly, and a poor man in shabby clothing also comes in, and you pay attention to the one who wears the fine clothing and say, "Have a seat here, please," while you say to the poor man, "Stand there," or, "Sit at my feet," have you not made distinctions among yourselves, and become judges with evil thoughts? Listen, my beloved brethren. Has not God chosen those who are poor in the world to be rich in faith and heirs of the kingdom which he has promised to those who love him? But you have dishonored the poor man. Is it not the rich who oppress you, is it not they who drag you into court? Is it not they who blaspheme the honorable name which was invoked over you?

Frequently we need to get back to basics. An old sea captain knew this, or at least the well-known story

says that he did. Every morning as he came up to
the quarterdeck, he systematically took a small key
from his pocket, opened a narrow drawer, removed
a slip of paper, gazed at it for an intense moment,
replaced the paper in the drawer, turned the lock,
tucked the key in his pocket, and went about his duties.

Through the years the first mate watched the ceremony—as regular in schedule, as precise in execution
as the changing of the guard at Buckingham Palace.
Finally the master retired and turned his keys over
to the first mate, who was to succeed him as captain.
With uncontrollable curiosity the new master bolted
to the quarterdeck, rifled through the keys, yanked
open the drawer, snatched at the paper—all the while
sure that he would discover some profound secret
of successful seamanship. His eyes devoured the two
simple sentences: "Left is port; right is starboard."

Every day the captain went back to the basics and
reminded himself which side of his ship was which.
We laugh at his need to review information so elemen-
tal, yet it may be the attention to the basic issues of
life that make the difference. Certainly for a captain,
inching his ship through a narrow entry into port to
remember which side is port and which is starboard
as he gives his commands to the helmsman is a matter
of vast importance to the ship, its cargo, and its crew.

A lesson in the basics of Christian living is what
James gave his hearers at the beginning of the second
chapter in his letter—a lesson in treating people right.
Along with our love for God and our trust in Jesus
Christ as Savior, dealing with our neighbor in love

is fundamental to who we are and what we do as Christians. Yet how hard it is for us to be consistent at this, and how hard it is for us even to recognize that we are not consistent in our treatment of those around us! Wisdom that works is what we need. In a graphic, memorable way James gives that to us.

Remember Where the Glory Belongs

Partiality is one of our great problems. The law of neighbor love is hard to keep because we find strong reasons for caring for some people while rejecting others. We are partial, prejudiced. We play favorites.

James left no doubt about what he meant by *partiality* in his command, "My brethren, show no partiality as you hold the faith of our Lord Jesus Christ, the Lord of glory" (2:1). Immediately he illustrated the attitude that was to be avoided: "For if a man with gold rings and in fine clothing comes into your assembly, and a poor man in shabby clothing also comes in, and you pay attention to the one who wears the fine clothing and say, 'Have a seat here, please,' while you say to the poor man, 'Stand there,' or 'Sit at my feet,' have you not made distinctions among yourselves, and become judges with evil thoughts?" (2:2–4).

Discrimination, even snobbery, seem to be the issue here. A person was fawned over merely because he had wealth and power. It is possible that the "gold rings" and the "fine clothing" indicate that the aristocrat may have been an official of the Roman empire,

perhaps one who was courting the Christians to gain
political support.

Whatever the precise circumstances, James found
the whole performance unworthy of true believers.
The church—here called "assembly" or "synagogue"—should have been the place where Christian
attitudes were cherished and Christian values prevailed. Yet here in the circle where grace was celebrated, where God's love for all persons was preached,
secular practices of partiality, preferential treatment
of some persons to the hurt of others, had crept in.

The need for wisdom to treat people right was obvious. James's first word of such wisdom came even
before he described their deplorable discrimination.
It is implied in his opening phrases, "My brethren,
show no partiality as you hold the faith of our Lord
Jesus Christ, the Lord of glory" (2:1). "Remember
where the glory belongs" was what James said here.
The New English Bible catches the point precisely: "My
brothers, believing as you do in our Lord Jesus Christ,
who reigns in glory, you must never show snobbery"
(2:1).

Jesus' own example rules out snobbery. He did not
live that way. In fact, there is much evidence that
he leaned over backwards to reach out to persons
who were demeaned and rejected by their society—
the tax collectors and the known sinners, for instance.
What was his praise of the widow who gave a penny?
Was it not a word of commendation to the poor who
worshiped God with all they had and a condemnation

of the wealthy who made a show of giving of their surplus (Mark 12:41-44)?

Since it is Jesus Christ who stands at the heart of our faith, our practices as Christians should be patterned on his. Secularity was a blight on the fruit of the church in James's day as it is in ours.

Jesus' own glory also rebukes our discrimination. What were James's friends doing? They were glorifying the wealthy and the powerful. They were giving glory where it was not due. Their teacher, drawing on his spiritual wisdom, had to remind them that there was no ultimate glory in material wealth or political prestige. The rich politicians were not lord; Jesus was. They had no true glory of their own; Jesus had it all.

His name and station as the "Lord Jesus Christ, the Lord of glory" make that plain. All of us who believe in him should know these basic truths. They are the port and the starboard of our ship of faith.

Remember What Discrimination Implies

James's second piece of wisdom is even more pointed than his first. It is found in the stinging words with which his description of partiality concludes: "Have you not made distinctions among yourselves, and become judges with evil thoughts?" (2:4). "Remember what discrimination implies" is the way we might paraphrase James's intent.

Discrimination makes us judges. James had already

warned about the harm that we do when we wrench the gavel of judgment from God's hands. As we discussed in Chapter 3, his warning was directed against our anger, which "does not work the righteousness [or the justice] of God" (1:20). When we become angry and damn others, we are trying to crowd God from the bench and sit in the judge's seat.

Discrimination, snobbery, partiality—these all tempt us to do the same thing. But when we become judges, we lose sight of ourselves as sinners. When we decide who is better than whom, we forget that we live only by God's grace, not by our wealth or righteousness. The "Lord Jesus Christ, the Lord of glory"—it is he to whom God has committed all judgment. If we believe in Christ's lordship, we also believe that to him alone belong the power and the right to judge.

Discrimination makes us bad judges. "Judges with evil thoughts," James branded his snobbish friends. They did not have the *authority* to judge; only Christ had that. And they did not have the *ability* to judge; they used false standards. Human judgment in spiritual matters almost always does. They violated one of the clearest and oldest principles of Scripture, a principle that the Lord announced to Samuel when he anointed David as Israel's king: "Do not look on his appearance or on the height of his stature [that is, of David's brother Eliab], because I have rejected him; for the Lord sees not as man sees; man looks on the outward appearance, but the Lord looks on the heart" (1 Sam. 16:7).

Undoubtedly, when pressed to give account for their show of discrimination, those early Christians could come up with their reasons: if we are good to these aristocrats we will have money to carry out our mission; if we treat them kindly, they may intervene on our behalf so that our suffering will be lightened. "Evil thoughts" James labeled such rationalizations. They involved evaluating people by external standards—always a dangerous pursuit.

Only Christ is a flawless judge; our attempts to take his place miscarry. When we discriminate in the church for reasons of wealth, status, race, or culture, we have strayed from one of the basic principles of the faith. We have confused ourselves with Christ and sought to usurp his lordship.

James's words are for us: Remember what discrimination implies. As we hear them, we ought sheepishly to hand the gavel back to the Lord of glory and slink penitently from the judge's chair. It does not fit us well, anyway.

Remember How Life Really Is

The final piece of wisdom that James brought focuses on the realities of life, which God's people were stupidly ignoring: "Listen, my beloved brethren. Has not God chosen those who are poor in the world to be rich in faith and heirs of the kingdom which he has promised to those who love him?" (2:5). Like Jesus and the Old Testament teachers of wisdom, James used a rhetorical question to make his point.

Some questions may have several answers. They are questions designed only to find out information. "Where are you going?" we ask. The answer may vary: "To bed," or, "To the store," or, "To San Francisco." It is a straightforward question. If, however, I ask, "You aren't going there, are you?" The question has a very different purpose. Its aim is not to ask but to state. It implies that the person should not go there. Its form carries its own answer. That is what a rhetorical question does.

"Has not God chosen those who are poor in the world to be rich in faith . . . ?" That was James's question. It carries its own answer: "Of course he has." In God's plan for life, *it is the poor who become rich;* Jesus said so. "Blessed are the poor in spirit, for theirs is the kingdom of heaven. . . . Blessed are those who are persecuted for righteousness' sake, for theirs is the kingdom of heaven" (Matt. 5:3, 10). Gold rings and fine clothing do not a kingdom make. That belongs to those who love God, regardless of their station.

And in the early church, there were many more poor than wealthy believers. That was part of God's surprise which helped God's people know how life really is: "For consider your call, brethren; not many of you were wise according to worldly standards, not many were powerful, not many were of noble birth; but God chose . . . what is low and despised in the world, even things that are not, to bring to nothing things that are, so that no human being might boast in the presence of God" (1 Cor. 1:26, 28–29).

Facing life as it really is means remembering that *the rich often afflict the poor* and, therefore, merit no special treatment: "But you have dishonored the poor man. Is it not the rich who oppress you, is it not they who drag you into court? Is it not they who blaspheme that honorable name by which you are called?" (2:6–7). Again rhetorical questions cue their own answers.

Unrealistic conduct, indeed! The Christians were flying in the teeth of God's will by dishonoring the poor whom God had chosen to honor and by courting members of the wealthy class who had made life miserable for believers.

James did not mean that those very citizens who were being lionized in the assembly were themselves the oppressors. He spoke to the matter of class. The Christians were showing favoritism to the wealthy just because they were of that class. Yet that was the very class who had harassed them in court by bringing false charges against them, and that was the social set who so often mocked and blasphemed the name of Christ, which Christians bore as the badge of their faith and baptism.

Wisdom to remember that Christ owned all life's glory, wisdom to remember that playing favorites meant playing judge, wisdom to remember that in God's plan the poor who loved him inherited a kingdom from which the godless rich were excluded— these were the basics that James printed in bold letters as daily reminders to his friends.

We would do well to set up a daily routine to take

them from the drawer of Scripture and read them anew morning by morning. To do so would not mean that all our sailing would be smooth. But it would help us to get our basic directions right, and that is no small thing.

5.

Wisdom to Keep God's Law

James 2:8-13

If you really fulfil the royal law, according to the scripture, "You shall love your neighbor as yourself," you do well. But if you show partiality, you commit sin, and are convicted by the law as transgressors. For whoever keeps the whole law but fails in one point has become guilty of all of it. For he who said, "Do not commit adultery," said also, "Do not kill." If you do not commit adultery but do kill, you have become a transgressor of the law. So speak and so act as those who are to be judged under the law of liberty. For judgment is without mercy to one who has shown no mercy; yet mercy triumphs over judgment.

Not all laws are equally important. Many of us learned that years ago from a clever feature carried in a national magazine. It was headed "It's the Law," or some such title. What it did, as you may recall, was to discover humorous, even silly laws, that were

still carried on the books of towns and cities across
the land.

My examples are not at all accurate, but they illus-
trate the kind of thing that we used to chuckle over:
it is against the law for a man with a peg-leg to dance
in a saloon in Cheyenne, Wyoming; it is against the
law for a horse to wear an umbrella while delivering
milk in Memphis, Tennessee; it is against the law to
drink lemonade in front of a church in Bimidji, Minne-
sota. And on they go—hundreds, if not thousands,
of statutes and ordinances that well-meaning public
servants voted into being for reasons now lost.

Not all laws are equally important. We learned that
from the ridiculous examples that tickled our funny
bones as children. We learned it in a more serious
setting when we were introduced to constitutional law
in our high school civics courses. There we found
out that laws enacted by townships or states could
be struck down in court if they violated our constitutional rights. The laws of the land, contained in the
United States Constitution and its amendments, took
priority over anything legislated by any legal body
in the country, including the Congress.

During the difficult days of the depression, we found
that out when the National Recovery Act (NRA) was
stricken from the books by the Supreme Court, even
though President Franklin Roosevelt and the Congress
supported it enthusiastically. Higher law prevailed;
lower law had to give way. The same thing happened,
even more dramatically, in 1954 when the Supreme
Court declared unconstitutional all legislation that had

created separate school systems for black students. The highest law—the Constitution as interpreted by the highest court—took precedence. All law in conflict with it had to give way, even if it took federal troops to make it happen.

Not all laws are equally important. But laws supported by our high courts are highly important. One of their main purposes is to protect human rights and to assure justice to all of us as citizens.

These high goals of law were not discovered at the time of the Magna Carta, which revolutionized British law in the thirteenth century. Nor were they invented in the eighteenth century when Jefferson, Madison, and others framed the American Constitution with its Bill of Rights.

The Bible is the source of the concern for justice and liberty that is embodied in our great Anglo-Saxon tradition of common law. From the time of Moses onward, the great spirits of the Bible stated and re-stated God's concern for human order, human freedom, human responsibility, human dignity. The Ten Commandments, the Sermon on the Mount, and the Letter of James all focus on the importance of doing God's will in relationship to neighbor—and even to enemy.

Failure in Love Hurts Our Neighbor

Behind law is love, the respect for the personhood and welfare of every human being because he or she is made by God and for him. At heart, law is for

God as much as for us. It is the means we use on earth to keep us from violating his will in heaven. Regard for law, especially law that respects and preserves the rights of every member of the human family, is a way of honoring God, whether we recognize it or not.

James went to great pains to urge his hearers to take the law of God with full seriousness. Part of his gift of wisdom to them as God's inspired spokesman was the wisdom to keep God's law.

What had bothered James were the reports that Christ's people, scattered throughout the Mediterranean world, had discriminated against the poor in favor of the rich. And they had done so in their very assembly, where the instruction of God should have prompted them to treat all persons with love and respect.

"If you really fulfil the royal law, according to the scripture, 'you shall love your neighbor as yourself,' you do well. But if you show partiality, you commit sin, and are convicted by the law as transgressors" (2:8–9). A failure in love—that is how James labels our partiality. It is a breach of the royal law—the law given by the King, the law kept by Jesus when he announced that God's kingdom had come, and the law that sets us free for kingly living.

We are dealing here with no trivial mistake when we act snobbishly toward the unfortunate. Our failure in love hurts our neighbor, and to inflict such hurt is sinful.

The origin of the law of neighbor love shows that.

Over all Israelite law there hovered the shadow of the Exodus. Who were the Israelites? They were slaves set free. What was their past? It was a history of mistreatment, of oppression, of discrimination, of lovelessness. Then God lifted them from that pit of slavery and made them his own people. But they were never to forget where they had come from and what they had been and how they had been treated. Their laws, given by God himself, were designed to make them different. Love was to be their law—love for neighbors and love for strangers: "The stranger who sojourns with you shall be to you as the native among you, and you shall love him as yourself; for you were strangers in the land of Egypt: I am the Lord your God" (Lev. 19:34).

That law convicts those who show prejudice. It convicts us by reminding us how much we need love and how much God, who is our Lord, has loved us. He did not discriminate against us when he saved us, and he specifically forbids us to discriminate against others: "You shall do no injustice in judgment; you shall not be partial to the poor or defer to the great, but in righteousness shall you judge your neighbor" (Lev. 19:15).

James left no doubt as to the guilt of some of the Christians: "But you have dishonored the poor man" (2:6). Those are pathetic words. In our kind of world poor men and women find honor hard to come by. Where wealth is admired, they feel left out; where achievement is praised, they are full of self blame. They have a hard enough time holding their heads up without us Christians saying to them "Stand there" or "Sit at my feet" (2:3).

Love—God's love, Christ's royal love, the Spirit's fruit of love—calls us to do better than that. And any time we do not, we show ourselves transgressors of God's law, deeply in need of his mercy.

Failure in Love Breaks the Whole Law of God

James, in bringing God's wisdom to us, wanted to undercut any possible excuses that we may bring to justify our loveless playing of favorites. One excuse that we might pose could be put like this: "Why all the fuss? We have kept all the other commandments, haven't we? Surely God will not be down on us for this one slight mistake?"

The answer that James gave brought that excuse to its knees: "For whoever keeps the whole law but fails in one point has become guilty of all of it. For he who said, 'Do not commit adultery,' said also, 'Do not kill.' If you do not commit adultery but do kill, you have become a transgressor of the law" (2:10–11).

A breach of law is an offense against God. That was the point. We should not think of the Ten Commandments or the Sermon on the Mount as mere collections of commandments. They are not magazine features which collect oddities in law from around the world. They are expressions of the will of the true and living God. To take any part lightly is to violate the whole. The law, in other words, is a unified expression of how God cares and what he wants. It is broken into sections only to help us remember and understand it. Failure to take any part seriously is an offense to him who is its author. An artist would be incensed at someone who stabbed his canvas. Even if only a portion were punctured, the whole painting would have been desecrated. So it is with God's law.

Prejudice against the poor is terrible. It attacks the will of God, and violates the law that he has given us for our own good.

Failure in Love Makes Us Liable to Judgment

Where sin is mentioned, judgment must always be in view. That is what God's will entails. To keep it brings blessing; it is a law of liberty. To break it— to fail to love as God calls us to—is to be liable to judgment: "So speak and so act as those who are to be judged under the law of liberty. For judgment is without mercy to one who has shown no mercy; yet mercy triumphs over judgment" (2:12-13).

Why are partiality and discrimination so dangerous? They hurt the neighbors that are their object. They break the law of God who wills good, not hurt, for our neighbor. And they face with the reality of judgment all who practice such partiality and discrimination.

The intensity of judgment depends on whether we have learned the lessons of mercy. Where mercy has been grasped as the law of life, we need fear no judgment: "Blessed are the merciful, for they shall obtain

mercy" (Matt. 5:7). "Mercy will triumph over judgment" is the way in which James paraphrased Jesus'
beatitude.

Where mercy is lacking, one thing is sure: we have
not truly learned that God is merciful. Where we have
beheld his mercy poured out to us in our abject poverty, we, in turn, will share that mercy with others.
God did not say to us "Stand there," or "Sit at my
feet." He took us in as full-fledged members of his
household. His mercy made us not his slaves but his
children.

When he did this, he wrote mercy into the fabric
of our universe. He inscribed it in his Scriptures as
the law of our lives. We are like the steward in Jesus'
parable who owed the king a vast debt. When he
begged for time to pay it, his master relented and
forgave the debt. No sooner had that happened than
his master found the servant trying to choke a very
small payment out of a fellow servant: "You wicked
servant!" the king shouted. "I forgave you all that
debt because you besought me; and should not you
have had mercy on your fellow servant, as I had mercy
on you?" (Matt. 18:32–33).

Judgment or mercy, those are our choices. We have
been loved by God in our poverty, and that love
teaches us to love others, especially those who are
poor and unfortunate. Our love for them is the best
way for us to demonstrate the way in which we have
learned life's great lesson—the lesson that God loved
us when we deserved only judgment.

To learn that lesson means that judgment need

never threaten us. God's mercy will see to that. Not to learn that lesson means that judgment will be our regular experience.

God cares too much about his own will and our own good to let us go unjudged. Neighbor love is no trite ordinance, no trivial statute to be cartooned on a page and smiled at by the fireside.

Not all laws are equally important. But God's law is royal. To live by it is to live like a king—and better. It is to live like a child of God, bathed in his mercies.

6.

Wisdom to Do
Good Works

James 2:14-26

What does it profit, my brethren, if a man says he has faith but has not works? Can his faith save him? If a brother or sister is ill-clad and in lack of daily food, and one of you says to them, "Go in peace, be warmed and filled," without giving them the things needed for the body, what does it profit?

So faith by itself, if it has no works, is dead.

But some one will say, "You have faith and I have works." Show me your faith apart from your works, and I by my works will show you my faith.

You believe that God is one; you do well. Even the demons believe—and shudder. Do you want to be shown, you shallow man, that faith apart from works is barren? Was not Abraham our father justified by works, when he offered his son Isaac upon the altar?

You see that faith was active along with his works, and faith was completed by works, and the scripture was fulfilled which says, "Abraham believed God, and it was reckoned

*to him as righteousness"; and he was called the friend of
God. You see that a man is justified by works and not by
faith alone. And in the same way was not also Rahab the
harlot justified by works when she received the messengers
and sent them out another way? For as the body apart
from the spirit is dead, so faith apart from works is dead.*

Strange things can happen in church. Part of the
Hubbard family lore, recounted and probably embel-
lished at our reunions, has to do with the unexpected
and the humorous happenings in church services.
There was the wedding, for instance, where my usually
reliable father confused the Twenty-third Psalm with
the marriage ceremony: "Dearly beloved," he intoned
with his customary kindly smile, "we are gathered
together in the sight of God and in the presence of
these *enemies.* . . ."
One of the strangest stories comes from our days
in the Methodist Church in Escalon, California, near
Stockton, where my father taught at the College of
the Pacific. Week by week we would drive the old
Franklin or Hudson the twenty miles to the country
town where my father preached. During a morning
sermon one Sunday, the service was disrupted by a
siren-sound which could only mean that the volunteer
fire crew was being summoned to duty. One by one
the men eased themselves from the pews and slipped
out the door. My father stuck to his sermon, fervently
determined to get the message across despite the dis-
tractions. What proved most puzzling was that the

buzzing alarm did not turn off, even though the volunteers had headed for the fire station.

Persistently it whined its message of warning throughout the church auditorium. The uneasiness among the congregation mounted. Surely conflagration must be threatening the whole town. Men and boys not on the crew edged out of the church as quietly and rapidly as possible to give a hand in the firefighting. When the alarm continued, my father closed the sermon ahead of schedule and rushed out the back door to see the catastrophe for himself.

What he found outside was a huddle of baffled men, who saw no fire and heard no alarm. Finally, my brother Paul, still in the church, solved the riddle: he sidled over to one of the members and turned off a brand-new hearing aid. Only then did the alarm cease, the men return from their "call" to duty, and the service continue. A new-fangled contraption—this happened about fifty years ago—had gone awry in church and provided many chuckles for the members of our family through the years.

The strange things that happen in church are not always humorous. Sometimes they approach the tragic. That was the case in some of the churches James addressed in his circular letter that made its way through the Mediterranean world. The strange thing that happened was a gross misunderstanding of something that should have been crystal-clear: Christians missed the meaning of the word *faith*—and not just the meaning of the word but the meaning of the act. What a basic mistake!

Faith is not just an intellectual concept; it is the basis of a true relationship with God. To miss its meaning has appalling results. In verse after verse James tried to drive that truth home. Faith wrongly defined, faith poorly lived, ends up being no faith. Here are James's own words on this: "What does it profit, my brethren, if a man says he has faith but has not works? . . . So faith by itself, if it has no works, is dead. . . . Do you want to be shown, you shallow man, that faith apart from works is barren?. . . . You see that a man is justified by works and not by faith alone. . . . For as the body apart from the spirit is dead, so faith apart from works is dead" (2:14, 17, 20, 24, 26).

There was no humor here. This was not a funny thing that happened in church. But it was strange— so strange that James attacked it with a cannonlike barrage of statements and questions. Profitless, barren, dead—those were the words used to describe faith which is misunderstood and misapplied.

And James left no doubt about what was missing— good works. Essentially his argument here continued the case he had been making throughout chapter two—the treatment of the poor. In fact we might see all of chapter two as an extended comment on the final verse of chapter one, where James described how our faith is to express itself: "Religion that is pure and undefiled before God and the Father is this: to visit orphans and widows in their affliction, and to keep oneself unstained from the world" (1:27).

Pure religion and true faith meant about the same

thing for James. They mean for us that the grace of
God has so gripped us with the truth of God's love
that love becomes the style of our lives. What were
we like when God demonstrated his love for us in
the death and resurrection of his Son? We were poor
and helpless, without power to save ourselves, without
the sense to return to the Father.

That is the message of the Bible: God loved us in
our unlovely condition; God saved us when we
seemed beyond rescue; God helped us in our helpless
estate. To believe that about us means to live that
way toward others.

In a word, the strange thing that had happened in
the churches for whom James felt responsible was this:
faith was defined and practiced without love. What
are the good works he insisted upon? They are works
of love—the consistent application of what he called
"the royal law": "You shall love your neighbor as
yourself" (2:8). In his driving argument, James made
two basic points about the connection of Christian
faith and love: (1) ceremony is no substitute for love;
(2) creed is no substitute for love.

Ceremony Is No Substitute for Love

James's illustration of where the churches had gone
wrong built on a common practice of the early church.
At the close of the weekly love-feast (communion service), the elders and deacons of the congregation
would offer words of peace to the members as they
departed for their homes.

This ritual was a reminder that God had made peace through the blood of Christ's cross and that Christ himself was their peace, who had made both Jew and Gentile into one people (Col. 1:20; Eph. 2:14). To be told to "depart in peace" was to be assured that all was well because God was on their side.

Yet this ceremony, significant though it was, was not enough: "If a brother or sister is ill-clad and in lack of daily food, and one of you says to them, 'Go in peace, be warmed and filled,' without giving them the things needed for the body, what does it profit? So faith by itself, if it has no works, is dead" (2:15–17). Lovelessness, even at communion, was apparently not uncommon in the early church. Remember how this contradiction staggered Paul: "When you meet together, it is not the Lord's supper that you eat. For in eating, each one goes ahead with his own meal, and one is hungry and another is drunk. What! Do you not have houses to eat and drink in? Or do you despise the church of God and humiliate those who have nothing? . . ." (1 Cor. 11:20–22).

Selfishness in the face of the body and blood of our Lord who offered himself selflessly for us all! Incredible! Yet true! Ceremony, even the holy communion and the ritual of extending Christ's peace to the people, is not a substitute for love. Indeed, the ceremony's point is to remind God's people of his love. But ceremony must be completed in our conduct. We have only grasped the meaning of the ceremony when we practice what it preaches in our own good works—our acts of selfless love.

Creed Is No Substitute for Love

The second illustration on which James based his argument had to do with the creedal beliefs of the people. Apparently they thought that they were all right as long as some of them believed accurately and others performed the works of love: "But some one will say, 'You have faith and I have works.' Show me your faith apart from your works, and I by my works will show you my faith. You believe that God is one; you do well. Even the demons believe—and shudder" (2:18–19).

Faith is intellectual, of course. There is a set of facts to be believed—facts about God and what he has done for us through Jesus Christ. But faith is more than acceptance of facts; it is also commitment to a Person who changes lives by setting them free to love others. Faith and love cannot be divided and parceled out through a congregation so that some members are believers and others are workers. Not all believe and love equally well. But all Christians must both believe and love. One without the other is incomplete—like a body without a spirit or a spirit without a body (2:26).

Note that James equated our faith with the body and our works of love with the spirit. Belief is the skeletal structure of our religion; it is our love for others that provides the life, the vitality, the energy to Christian discipleship.

Creeds cannot take the place of love, any more than there can be true Christian love without an understanding of how God has loved us through Jesus Christ. The Christians—both Jews and Gentiles—were loyal to the belief that there is only one true God, and they were proud of their loyalty. The Jewish Christians delighted in their constancy of faith which had linked them to the essential Jewish creed: "Hear, O Israel: The Lord our God is one Lord" (Deut. 6:4). The Gentile Christians eagerly renounced the paganism of their forefathers and endorsed the Jewish creed.

Both groups, now united in the churches, celebrated their orthodoxy with great enthusiasm. They had shunned the polytheistic superstitions of the pagan world that surrounded them and committed themselves to faith in the God of Abraham and Jesus. James's response to their creedal loyalty must have stunned them: "Even the demons believe—and shudder" (2:19). If intellectual orthodoxy is what faith means, the devil and his hordes are champions of orthodoxy. They well know who God is, what he has done, and what he wants from us. And they tremble before his majesty and power.

But they are not believers. And they are not believers because they are not lovers. Their rebellion has made them incapable of the good works by which true faith, saving faith, vital faith, fruitful faith is demonstrated.

James clinched his argument by citing two Old Testament examples, whose lives had often been used by the early Christian teachers to underscore the importance of faith: Abraham and Rahab. Both trusted God in godless contexts, but both showed how concrete their faith was by strong acts of obedience to God's command: "Was not Abraham our father justified by works, when he offered his son Isaac upon the altar? You see that faith was active along with his works, and faith was completed by works" (2:21–22). It was this combination of faith and works which qualified Abraham to be called "the friend of God" (2:23). "And in the same way was not also Rahab the harlot justified by works when she received the messengers and sent them out another way?" (2:25). Rahab showed her response to God's will by specific acts of care and concern in protecting the Israelite spies who had infiltrated her home city, Jericho.

Strange things can happen in church. There, of all places, we can miss the meaning of faith by severing it from love.

Yet even stranger things can happen. In church, when we truly hear God's word of wisdom—and do it—we can become living letters on which is written, for all the world to see, the strangest message of all: God has loved us as we are through Jesus Christ our Lord.

7.

Wisdom to Guard
Our Tongues

James 3:1-12

Let not many of you become teachers, my brethren, for you know that we who teach shall be judged with greater strictness. For we all make many mistakes, and if any one makes no mistakes in what he says he is a perfect man, able to bridle the whole body also. If we put bits into the mouths of horses that they may obey us, we guide their whole bodies. Look at the ships also; though they are so great and are driven by strong winds, they are guided by a very small rudder wherever the will of the pilot directs. So the tongue is a little member and boasts of great things. How great a forest is set ablaze by a small fire!

And the tongue is a fire. The tongue is an unrighteous world among our members, staining the whole body, setting on fire the cycle of nature, and set on fire by hell. For every kind of beast and bird, of reptile and sea creature, can be tamed and has been tamed by humankind, but no human being can tame the tongue—a restless evil, full of deadly poison. With it we bless the Lord and Father, and with it

we curse men, who are made in the likeness of God. From
the same mouth come blessing and cursing. My brethren,
this ought not to be so. Does a spring pour forth from the
same opening fresh water and brackish? Can a fig tree,
my brethren, yield olives, or a grapevine figs? No more can
salt water yield fresh.

Teachers and their tongues—that is our theme. Two
contrasting scenes come to my mind as I say those
words. The scenes are brightly lighted in my memory,
like a sound-stage set up for color television, though
they happened decades ago.

One scene took place at Westmont College, where
I spent my last two years of undergraduate study. I
had just arrived to begin my junior year. My brother
John had been there for some years, teaching music.
At one of the welcoming parties or receptions, I met
a professor who worked with my brother. I was delighted to meet her, until she asked me a question:
Do you play the piano like your brother? I nervously
shook my head and mumbled something about plunk-
ing a few chords now and then but not playing well.
Her face clouded—and so did mine—as she re-
sponded: Too bad you have no talent!

Teachers and their tongues—the power to wound
and the power to bless. I do not want to be overdra-
matic. I survived that sharp and cutting statement,
which I am sure the piano instructor did not mean
to have come out the way it sounded.

One of the reasons that I did survive was an earlier

conversation—in junior high school—with another teacher. She was my English instructor and the counselor for our eighth-grade class. She asked me to stay after school one day, and she told me things that changed my life. "You get your work done quickly," she began. "That shows you have a good mind. But I feel that you waste your time reading books that will not do you much good." I blushed, knowing she was right. Escape literature furnished much of my diet in those years. I had traveled the wildernesses of the north with all the great dogs like *Shag, Dog of the Timberline.* I had mushed behind every sled that ever plowed through the Yukon snows to the Alaskan gold rush. I was all ears, as she continued: "If you really want to use your talent and make something of your life, I am willing to help. You read the books I recommend, and then you and I can discuss them."

That vote of confidence was a turning point in my life. I began to take myself and my talents with more seriousness. My reading and thinking patterns changed, and my life during the thirty-five years since has been immeasurably enriched.

The power of a teacher's tongue—that is one of life's great realities. With directness and perception, James spoke to this matter: "Let not many of you become teachers, my brethren, for you know that we who teach shall be judged with greater strictness. For we all make many mistakes, and if any one makes no mistakes in what he says he is a perfect man, able to bridle the whole body also" (3:1–2). Apparently some of the Christians were rushing into a ministry of teaching in a way that seemed rash to James. Why they were so eager to teach we cannot be sure. Certainly teachers were needed in a society where only a minority could read, where few copies of the Old Testament existed, and where the New Testament had not yet been completed. Teachers had prestige then as now, and some persons may have been eager for the recognition that came with the office. Teachers in the Christian assemblies had a rank and significance akin to that of rabbi in the Jewish synagogue. Beyond that, teachers in the early church had the right to be supported by the congregation, as the apostle Paul made clear: "If we have sown spiritual good among you, is it too much if we reap your material benefits? . . . Do you not know that those who are employed in the temple service get their food from the temple, and those who serve at the altar share in the sacrificial offerings? In the same way, the Lord commanded that those who proclaim the gospel should get their living by the gospel" (1 Cor. 9:11, 13–14).

In those early decades of the church that formed the setting for James's circular letter, there was little formal training and little examination of credentials for teachers. Those who felt they had the gift would begin to teach, and, if they could persuade others to hear them, they could assume the teacher's role.

Teachers Face the Greater Judgment

James's warning was well taken. The teacher's office was not to be sought lightly or entered rashly, for two reasons: (1) teachers face greater judgment than others; (2) teachers make larger mistakes than the rest of God's people.

"We who teach shall be judged with greater strictness." That one sentence spoke volumes. It reminded James's friends that greater privilege carried with it greater responsibility. Wherever people look to us for leadership, there we have great opportunity to hurt them. They have literally put their spiritual, mental, and emotional welfare in our hands. That is a weighty burden to carry. We must handle it with care.

Teaching is exciting work. I know few experiences more exhilarating than to have eager, open faces hanging on my words. To see pens taking notes on every sentence, hands waving enthusiastically to signal an apt comment or a tough question, and students crowding around the rostrum after class to clarify fine points or to report their progress on assignments is heady stuff, even now with all the educational resources of the late twentieth century.

Think what the situation must have been like in the early churches. The eagerness to learn must have been overwhelming. Jews wanted to gain fresh understanding of their Scriptures and how they pointed to the coming of Jesus. Gentiles wanted to learn biblical history so that the covenants and promises could become their own. Both Jews and Gentiles hung on every word of Jesus' life and teachings. New converts craved to learn the basics of the faith so that they could be baptized into full membership.

Many of God's people—perhaps too many—rushed to become teachers. And they had some freedom both in serving as teachers and in what they taught. There were no set curricula and no methods of inspection. From town to town and congregation to congregation, teachers could teach what they chose unless reports of their errors brought some kind of visit from an apostle or his representative.

It took a good bit of maturity to minister under such circumstances. Brightness and quickness alone were not enough. A *ready tongue* could be as much of a liability as an asset. It had to be matched by a *controlled tongue,* which indeed usually signified the kind of restraint and discipline over all of life that a teacher should have.

James's note was well taken: when a person has his tongue in check, the chances are good that this verbal maturity has spread to the rest of his person (3:2). It may have been something like this that Paul had in mind when he linked "pastors and teachers" as one office in his list of spiritual callings in the church (Eph. 4:11).

Teaching is not a discipline isolated from the total care of people. We teach best out of our experience in the hurts and failings, the joys and triumphs, of our pupils. And only those mature enough to handle full pastoral responsibility are mature enough to teach. The stakes are too high, the risks too great, and the judgment too perilous to allow anything else.

Teachers Make the Larger Mistakes

After his main point—"Let not many of you become teachers"—James centered on the dangers of teaching, dependent as it is on the use of the tongue. Few passages in Scripture are more blunt in detailing both the power and the danger of human speech.

The tongue is so powerful it guides the rest of the personality. Long before Sigmund Freud taught us that slips of the tongue were clues to our inner feelings, James perceived the intimate connection between what we say and what we are.

Speech is a key to our humanity. Our skeletal frame is not unlike other primates. Some mammals, like whales or dolphins, bear resemblances to us in size of brain. The instincts of many higher animals make them more sensitive to their environments and alert to danger than we are. But no research has yet revealed any system of communication as elaborate, as advanced, as effective as human speech. It is the spoken word that—for good or evil—most clearly expresses what we are and feel as human beings.

James illustrated the power of the tongue with three graphic figures of speech. The tongue is as powerful as *a horse's bit:* "If we put bits into the mouths of horses that they may obey us, we guide their whole bodies" (3:3). The tongue is also as powerful as *a ship's rudder:* "Look at the ships also; though they are so great and are driven by strong winds, they are guided by a very small rudder wherever the will of the pilot directs" (3:4). It may not be out of place to read into these illustrations pictures of the church. The church is compared both to a body and a ship. The teacher within the church could then be compared to the bit or the rudder, because it is the teacher, who, under Christ—the Head of the body and the Captain of the ship—guides and steers the congregation in its spiritual directions. The tongue is also compared to *a dangerous fire:* "So the tongue is a little member and boasts of great things. How great a forest is set ablaze by a small fire!" (3:5).

The tongue is so wayward it is impossible to tame. James used this argument to underscore his point: "Let not many of you become teachers." Maturity in speech comes slowly, and mastery of the tongue is impossible. Those were his stern observations. The conclusion was clear: Do not become a teacher unless God has given you the wisdom to deal with the dangers of the tongue: "And the tongue is a fire. The tongue is an unrighteous world among our members, staining the whole body, setting on fire the cycle of nature, and set on fire by hell" (3:6).

The words were strong, and we have to grapple with their meaning. The whole personality has been stained by sin, we know that from all of Scripture. It was not just Adam's *tongue* that fell in the beginning; it was his whole person. But nothing reveals our fallen nature so quickly and so consistently as our tongue; it does stain the whole body, as its thoughtless or ruthless comments bubble out. It does spread its heat like a forest fire on the world, and especially the people, around us (James called it "the cycle of nature"). And it does smoke with the very cinders of hell, so devilish is its performance much of the time: "For every kind of beast and bird, of reptile and sea creature, can be tamed and has been tamed by humankind, but no human being can tame the tongue—a restless evil, full of deadly poison" (3:7–8).

A clear illustration of our untamable tongues is the fact that we speak out of both sides of it. We use it positively and negatively at once: "With it we bless the Lord and Father, and with it we curse men, who are made in the likeness of God" (3:9). This hypocrisy shows how out of line we are with God's purposes: his springs do not gush forth both fresh water and brackish; his sweet fig trees do not yield bitter olives; his tart grape vines do not yield sugary figs; the salt water of the Dead Sea does not give forth the sweet water of a mountain stream (3:11–12).

Wisdom is what we need—wisdom to guard our tongues, especially if we are called to teach others. I began with two scenes that had affected my life for bad and good. I began with those stories because I did not dare face the harm that I personally may have done to my own students.

What should we do in light of the heavy responsibility of the teacher and the boundless power of the tongue? We should *prayerfully support those who do Christ's teaching* in his church, knowing full well the weight of ministry that is theirs. We should also *thoughtfully consider our own calling* as to whether God has equipped us for such responsibilities by giving us the maturity and discipline to handle them. Finally, we should *daily dedicate our tongues to Christ's loving service,* realizing that he alone has the power to tame the untamable.

8.

Wisdom to Get Along with Each Other

James 3:13-18

Who is wise and understanding among you? By his good life let him show his works in the meekness of wisdom. But if you have bitter jealousy and selfish ambition in your hearts, do not boast and be false to the truth. This wisdom is not such as comes down from above, but is earthly, unspiritual, devilish. For where jealousy and selfish ambition exist, there will be disorder and every vile practice. But the wisdom from above is first pure, then peaceable, gentle, open to reason, full of mercy and good fruits, without uncertainty or insincerity. And the harvest of righteousness is sown in peace by those who make peace.

Every teacher has had the experience many times. A student in the third row squirms a little as though the seat of the chair were lined with cactus shoots. Then gradually gaining courage, he peeks out from behind the heads of the students in front of him.

Slowly, as though raised by a rusty winch, he raises his hand. So hesitant are the movements that the teacher is not sure at first whether the student is signaling a question or scratching his ear.

Finally as the hand goes up its last six inches and quavers shyly, the uncertainty fades, and the teacher calls on the student. Stammered out, the first words are predictable. The teacher fights the temptation to wince as he hears them: "This may be a stupid question, but—"

We let the rest of the question trail off, because the main point has already been made. Another nervous, fearful student has made a powerful statement about teaching and learning. Of course the student has said something about himself—his lack of confidence, his uncertainty about the subject, his fear of laughter among his classmates. But much more than that, the shaky introduction to his question has betrayed his opinion of teachers. Somewhere along the line he has met men and women who used their knowledge to manipulate or to humiliate others.

That hesitant preface—"This may be a stupid question, but . . ."—is like a leather shield held up to parry the jabbing arrows of an insensitive teacher. To be smart or clever is not qualification enough for a ministry of teaching. Quickness and brightness by themselves make dangerous weapons. They batter students with statements like, "Now that's a stupid question if I ever heard one," or needle them before their friends with lines like "Did you hear what Charlie just asked?"

The Apostle James shuddered over just that kind of teaching. One of his strong concerns was that persons without proper qualifications were striving to become teachers in the churches. He pulled no punches in branding this ambition as wrong: "Let not many of you become teachers, my brethren, for you know that we who teach shall be judged with greater strictness" (3:1). Persons whose tongues are not tamed by spiritual discipline should not think that they are gifted for and called to teaching. That was the burden of James's argument.

As his letter continued, James seemed to anticipate the objections of his hearers, especially the self-appointed teachers. "But, James," we can almost hear them say, "we are learned in biblical matters; we have facile tongues and are able to answer questions readily; besides, we have gathered a group of students around us who hang on our every word." James was not intimidated by their objections. His picture of what made for bad and good teaching was clear. He understood well the difference between cleverness and wisdom, and he knew fully that much of what passed for wisdom in human society deserved other names—shrewdness, cunning, craftiness.

James answered the arguments of the ambitious teachers in a time-honored biblical way. He drew sharp contrasts between the wrong and the right kinds of wisdom. Psalm 1 compared the fruitful life of those who obey God's law with the chafflike existence of the ungodly. Jesus set two houses side by side for comparison—one built on a foundation of sand, the other built on a base of solid rock (Matt. 7). Paul painted the sharp differences between the work which human flesh does and the fruit which the divine Spirit grows (Gal. 5). In the same way James held up two kinds of wisdom—one earthly and one heavenly—and showed how vastly different they were.

The Cleverness That Divides

The earthly brand of wisdom is not really wisdom at all. It is what we mistake for wisdom when we do not recognize the real thing. Cleverness would be a more apt name for it. It may be quick and bright, it may have flash and fire, but it is not good. It is not a wisdom that helps people get along together; it is a cleverness that divides them into factions.

How is this cleverness demonstrated? This was how James saw it: "But if you have bitter jealousy and selfish ambition in your hearts, do not boast and be false to the truth" (3:14). And again, "For where jealousy and selfish ambition exist, there will be disorder and every vile practice" (3:16). Jealousy and ambition—those are the ugly forms in which this cleverness shows itself.

Think a minute about what this means. James had teachers in mind, or, more precisely, those who wanted to be teachers. What were teachers supposed to do? They were to help their students understand the meaning of the Christian faith—its teachings about God and its demands on their lives. They failed at two points: (1) they could not help students because they had their eyes on themselves—jealousy and ambition leave us no room to think about others; (2) they could not teach the Christian faith because their lives denied its basic message—jealousy and ambition are opposites of the love and service which Jesus embodied.

Cleverness was spending its energies not to nurture students but to increase the status of the teacher. Competition had crowded out love; aggressiveness had pushed grace to the side. "If you live that way," James warned, "do not call yourselves teachers, do not boast of your wisdom. If you do, you are being 'false to the truth' (3:14). Your life cancels out your words and makes liars out of you."

How is this cleverness described? James reserved sharp language for it: "This wisdom is not such as comes down from above, but is earthly, unspiritual, devilish (3:15)." What a jolting indictment this was. Here were the leaders of various congregations rejoicing in the intellectual powers that they had, perhaps even thanking God for them. Yet they were dead wrong. Their supposed gifts were not at all from God: theirs was not a wisdom from above; it was a cleverness from below.

Earthly, James called it, because it smacked of the base selfishness so typical of our fallen human nature. Cleverness is what people admire and practice who have no perspective beyond this world. It is an animal-like drive for survival at any cost. It is so earthbound that it neither rejoices in God's love nor fears God's judgment.

Unspiritual was another term that James used of this cleverness that sets people against each other. "Soulless" could be another translation. It means life on the purely human plain, limited to the resources of human instinct and ingenuity, and marked by dullness and blindness to all spiritual matters.

Devilish was the word by which James took his criticism one step further. "Demonlike" is the literal meaning. How do the devil and his troops operate? They try to take our minds off the Lord; they try to set God's people against each other in envy and strife; they urge us to do things our way and to lean on our own resources; they push us to use our power in ways that hurt others.

How does cleverness work out? "Disorder and every vile practice" was the phrase chosen to express the outcome. What else could we expect? Jealousy and ambition sour any situation into which they are injected. They set neighbor against neighbor and lead to disorder. If every person is for himself, only anarchy can result, with all of the hatred, fear, suspicion, and intrigue that anarchy entails.

One of my friends began his career in a lumber camp. At one of his first meals he began to reach for an orange on the fruit plate. The corner of his eye caught the silver gleam of a fork that was about to sink into his outstretched hand. When he jerked it out of the way, the old logger next to him menaced him with the fork, and told him in the salty language of the timbermen that he was to ask for the orange, not to take it. Even that rough setting had shown that respect for the rights of others and simple rules of courtesy were essential. Even at the loggers' table, the law could not be every man for himself. Order had to prevail or life would become intolerable. That was James's point. Cleverness led to a selfish disorder that disrupted all Christian fellowship.

The Wisdom That Unites

James was not content with exposing the evil of divisive cleverness; he took great delight in showing the better way—the way of the wisdom that draws God's people together.

How is this wisdom demonstrated? James began with that question and answered it himself: "Who is wise and understanding among you? By his good life let him show his works in the meekness of wisdom" (3:13). We can catch the contrast between this and the jealousy and ambition which cleverness displays. Not smart words but good life, not aggressive competition but meekness are the badges of wisdom. There is a wholeness to true wisdom that brings heart and head, feelings and thoughts, deeds and words together.

Not just brilliance to teach with words, but the strong gentleness (meekness) to serve others is the qualification of the truly wise person, the person fit to teach the people of God.

How is this wisdom described? The wise person listens to James's earlier words that deal with anger and vindictiveness: "Let every man be quick to hear, slow to speak, slow to anger," and "receive with meekness the implanted word, which is able to save your souls" (1:19, 21). Hearing the word, receiving it with meekness, is the key to mature wisdom. And the phrase *the implanted word* should be stressed. The word has become part of us and begun to change our characters.

When it has, James's description begins to come true: "But the wisdom from above is first pure, then peaceable, gentle, open to reason, full of mercy and good fruits, without uncertainty or insincerity" (3:17). Those are the attributes we admire and long for. Would not that be a happy list of things to hear said about one of us at a retirement party? They bear a closer look: *pure* means free from the defilements of jealousy and ambition that stain the lives of the clever; *peaceable* suggests the ability to maintain composure even under hostile or anger-provoking circumstances; *open to reason* describes a sensitivity to the other person's point of view and flexibility to change one's own mind when the evidence indicates; *full of mercy and good fruits* points to a disposition of love and compassion that reach out to the needs of the struggling; *without uncertainty* is a way of picturing a loyalty to God that does not waver in its commitment; *without insincerity* indicates a freedom from the hypocrisy that pretends to do what it does not, to be what it is not, and to care when it cannot.

Who can vote against any point on that list? Who of us would not want to have teachers who fit that description? Who would not want to be able to live that way?

How is this wisdom discovered? From above, was James's answer. Here he followed in Job's train. Job described the process by which we find and mine gold, silver, iron, copper, and precious stones.

> "But where shall wisdom be found?
>   And where is the place of understanding?"
>   *Job 28:12*

The answer is not with humankind, but with God:

> "God understands the way to it,
>   and he knows its place.
> . . . .
> And he said to man,
> 'Behold, the fear of the Lord, that is wisdom;
>   and to depart from evil is understanding.' "
>   *Job 28:23, 28*

From above, from knowing and fearing God, true Christian teachers and true Christian disciples are made.

What is most remarkable about this wisdom from above is that it came down to us in a form, in a Person we can understand. It was the greatest Wise Man, the noblest Teacher, who said: "Take my yoke upon you, and learn from me; for I am gentle and lowly in heart, and you will find rest for your souls" (Matt. 11:29). That Teacher, with his wisdom from above, welcomes all our questions, even those we may be tempted to call stupid.

9.

Wisdom to Resist Temptation

James 4:1-10

What causes wars, and what causes fightings among you? Is it not your passions that are at war in your members? You desire and do not have; so you kill. And you covet and cannot obtain; so you fight and wage war. You do not have, because you do not ask. You ask and do not receive, because you ask wrongly, to spend it on your passions. Unfaithful creatures! Do you not know that friendship with the world is enmity with God? Therefore whoever wishes to be a friend of the world makes himself an enemy of God. Or do you suppose it is in vain that the scripture says, "He yearns jealously over the spirit which he has made to dwell in us"? But he gives more grace; therefore it says, "God opposes the proud, but gives grace to the humble." Submit yourselves therefore to God. Resist the devil and he will flee from you. Draw near to God and he will draw near to you. Cleanse your hands, you sinners, and purify your hearts, you men of double mind. Be wretched and mourn and weep. Let your laughter be turned to mourning and your joy to dejection. Humble yourselves before the Lord and he will exalt you.

It happened recently at the University of Pittsburgh. Students were peacefully chatting in one of the academic buildings. It was a scene of serenity and calm. Quiet voices, gentle laughter, rustling pages of busy readers were the only disturbance. Then a massive blast shook the campus. Walls toppled, roofs caved in, plate glass was shattered. A cluster of people were wounded, and a couple were dead.

Natural gas had been ignited accidentally and a peaceful quadrangle had been turned into a holocaust. The staggering sound and the shocking sight had all the impact of a battle on those who saw it. The gas that should have kept the students warm turned cruelly destructive in a split second.

The transition from chapter three to chapter four in the Letter of James has an impact almost as startling. His description of the wisdom from above and the lives of those who possess it was as tranquil as a spring day by a quiet pond. Peace and righteousness had been his theme: "And the harvest of righteousness is sown in peace by those who make peace" (3:18). Like their Master, wise Christians are peacemakers. They take seriously his promise: "Blessed are the peacemakers, for they shall be called sons of God" (Matt. 5:9). If our concern is for righteousness in a fallen, broken, marred world, then anger, hostility, and rashness are not the way to get it. Nor is the clever cunning of arrogant teachers whose brightness outshines their goodness. Righteousness is only harvested when it is sown in peace by those whose aim is to make peace. That was God's program for changing the world, as James saw it.

But in the next verse the whole scene exploded. Not peace but war was the real state of the churches: "What causes wars, and what causes fightings among you? Is it not your passions that are at war in your members? You desire and do not have; so you kill. And you covet and cannot obtain; so you fight and wage war. You do not have, because you do not ask. You ask and do not receive, because you ask wrongly, to spend it on your passions" (4:1-3). These were blasting words, shattering the complacency of people who thought they were living a sheltered existence. They had succumbed to all manner of temptation and hardly known what or why. It took James's shocking words to rock them from their complacency.

What We Need to Recognize Temptation

Wars, fightings, passions, killing—these are startling terms to use of Christian congregations. But James knew that Christians are not angels; they are human beings. The moods, attitudes, and methods of the world do not always stop at the door of the church. Facing our temptations as Christians takes wisdom from above—and in large measure. Three commands to help us deal with the temptations that plague our human nature can be distilled from James' words: (1) be aware that temptation breeds hostility; (2) be alert to what causes us to sin; (3) be informed of the dangers of worldliness.

Be aware that temptation breeds hostility. Almost without knowing it, the Lord's people were at war with one another. The loving support that should have been their way of life had been eroded, chipped away by a thousand mindless conflicts. What should have been a close-knit community had become a sadly shattered battleground.

Both lust and guilt lead to such hostility. Lust makes us hostile because we are angry with those who have what we want. We resent their successes— the fine home, the prominent job, the beautiful wife, the large salary. Envy makes us hostile. It also may start wars among us by encouraging us to try to take what belongs to someone else or to cheat to get what we want. Any or all of those actions set person against person, neighbor against neighbor, friend against friend. Any activity that has such bitter results has to be wrong.

Guilt, too, makes us hostile unless we own up to it. We carry it like a chafing burden that makes us sore all over. One usual response to guilt is to blame others for our faults. And that blame merely fuels the fires of hostility. Guilt feelings have started as many personal wars as any emotions I can think of.

Temptation is not to be toyed with. It not only rattles our insides when we succumb to it; it sets up rumblings throughout our neighborhoods. Family, friends, and fellow Christians all become casualties of such warfare.

Be alert to what causes us to sin. One of the reasons that sin can creep up on us and ensnare us is that we do not pay attention to how it works. James had made a point of warning his audience earlier. When they gave in to anger or doubt, they tried to blame God for their sin; after all, it was he who controlled their circumstances. Wisdom to know how sin works was one gift James had to give them: "But each person is tempted when he is lured and enticed by his own desire. Then desire when it has conceived gives birth to sin; and sin when it is full-grown brings forth death" (1:14–15). Sin is like a seduction. It starts with desire and ends in pregnancy. Each step leads inevitably and imperceptibly to the next—except that the child sin produces is death. It was the impact of sin on the sinner that James described in the earlier passage.

In chapter four James described the other side of sin's effect—the damage done by it to the community. Again the cycle began with passion or desire: "you desire and do not have; so you kill" (4:2). The lust for what we do not have is a direct insult to God. It says to God that he has not been good to us, that he does not know what is best. When we are not content with what he gives, all kinds of bad things happen. Our dissatisfaction drives us to take what we want when we want or to smolder with frustration when we do not get it. Apparently the frustration among James's friends rose to the point where they

were willing even to kill to get their way. Whether
this was literally true we do not know. But the language suggests that their greed was so great that they
were willing to see others badly damaged to get their
way: "And you covet and cannot obtain; so you fight
and wage war" (4:2).

Sin, the desire that had seemed like a nice, harmless
wish, led to conflict that turned the church into a disaster area. James was not specific about the precise nature of the desire. Perhaps wealth or power were its
most likely objects. In the struggle with their wealthy,
powerful opponents the young Christians thought they
could triumph if they had the same advantages their
opponents had.

They even prayed, though not with the right motive, that God would grant their desires: ". . . You
do not have, because you do not ask. You ask and
do not receive, because you ask wrongly, to spend
it on your passions" (4:2–3). They had tried to pretend
that they wanted more of the goods of this world in
order to serve God better. God knew that their mo-
tives, in fact, were their own pleasure, and he denied
their requests. Desire for the wrong things or for the
right things for the wrong reasons—that is the subtle
method that sin uses to take charge of our lives.

Be informed of the dangers of worldliness. That was
James's final warning: "Unfaithful creatures! Do you
not know that friendship with the world is enmity
with God? Therefore whoever wishes to be a friend
of the world makes himself an enemy of God" (4:4).
War among the members and infidelity to God—those

were the fruit of their lusts. Dissatisfaction with our lots, desire to have what others have, passion to feed our own pleasure—those are all worldly ways. To vote for them is to vote against God; to embrace them is to thrust God aside; to pursue them is to play false with God. James called those who yield to that temptation guilty of adultery.

There was no "harvest of righteousness" in that scene. James must have been pained as he surveyed the rubble. The people called to be peacemakers were wracked by warfare; the people called to be Christ's bride were shamed by infidelity. They had failed to recognize temptation for what it is, and, consequently, they had succumbed to its lures and reaped its bloody results.

What We Need to Resist Temptation

Two encouraging thoughts brightened the picture for James as he surveyed the damage done by sin: (1) God's grace was yet available; (2) human nature could still be changed. Temptation was not the ultimate winner. Disaster areas could be cleared and rebuilt. God's people could learn to resist temptation by remembering the lessons of grace and the actions of obedience.

Remember the lessons of grace. God may express his care for us in judgment when we violate his purposes, but grace is what he prefers to demonstrate: "Or do you suppose it is in vain that the scripture says, 'He yearns jealously over the spirit which he has made to dwell in us'? But he gives more grace; therefore it says, 'God opposes the proud, but gives grace to the humble' " (4:5–6). He wants our loyalty; after all, he made us. And he is willing to give us grace to make us loyal. More than anything else he wants us to acknowledge that we need that grace. That is probably the best definition of humility: the constant awareness that without God's grace we do nothing and are nothing.

Remember the actions of obedience. That was the urgent word with which James closed this section of his letter. Understanding God's grace must always lead to action on the part of his people. The Christian life is not passive sitting or sleeping. It is active standing, walking, running. Our power and our status come from God's grace; we have nothing on our own. Yet there are steps we must take in the battle against temptation. In rapid succession, James outlined them.

"Submit yourselves therefore to God" (4:7). Covetousness was not God's plan, and warfare was not his will. In both the seed and the fruit of sin, lack of submission was evident. God's people had to turn from their independence and again acknowledge God's lordship. How can we count on his power and grace without that?

"Resist the devil and he will flee from you" (4:7). Where lust and envy lurk, the devil is at hand. Not to recognize this threat is foolishness. Yet to think that the devil is irresistible is equally foolish. God's grace is more than a match for him. When we claim that grace to strengthen us in temptation, Satan has no choice but to flee. He knows when he is beaten. James has already told us how the devil's legions shudder before the power of the one true God (2:19).

"Draw near to God and he will draw near to you" (4:8). God is at hand to meet us in our need. We draw near by acknowledging how much we need him. The distance between us and God is not geographical; it is spiritual. He is already by our sides, but we do not know that until we ask his help.

"Cleanse your hands, you sinners, and purify your hearts, you men of double mind" (4:8). The double command was well taken. The warlike aggressiveness had defiled the hands of the Christians. They had wounded, perhaps killed others, in their selfish ambition. And the pure hearts were necessary because of their divided loyalties: they tried to serve God while driven to seek their own gain.

"Be wretched and mourn and weep" (4:9). Only true repentance will signal our seriousness to God and to ourselves. It is the mourners who will receive comfort, as Jesus promised (Matt. 5:4). Angry lust or foolish glee had been their dispositions. Neither of these paid enough attention to God's holiness or their own failures.

"Humble yourselves before the Lord and he will exalt you" (4:10). Exaltation, power, prestige were their desires. They lusted for them to the point of war. That was the wrong way. We gain height by bowing down; we stoop in order to conquer. That is the biblical pattern.

"The harvest of righteousness is sown in peace"

(3:18). That is God's pattern for our welfare. Envy and lust are constant temptations. We seem bent to want what we should not have. Our desires are like the fuel that can peacefully warm our cold bodies or angrily blow up our buildings. When our desires are directed toward and by God's grace, peace and righteousness will warm God's people to their centers. When that desire lusts for our gain, the results are menacingly explosive. The Pittsburgh students seem to have had no choice. But with us it is different. Every day we cast our votes—for war or peace.

10.

Wisdom to Avoid Presumptuousness

James 4:11-17

Do not speak evil against one another, brethren. He that speaks evil against a brother or judges his brother, speaks evil against the law and judges the law. But if you judge the law, you are not a doer of the law but a judge. There is one lawgiver and judge, he who is able to save and to destroy. But who are you that you judge your neighbor?

Come now, you who say, "Today or tomorrow we will go into such and such a town and spend a year there and trade and get gain"; whereas you do not know about tomorrow. What is your life? For you are a mist that appears for a little time and then vanishes. Instead you ought to say, "If the Lord wills, we shall live and we shall do this or that." As it is, you boast in your arrogance. All such boasting is evil. Whoever knows what is right to do and fails to do it, for him it is sin.

The text for this chapter is one of the most important statements in the Bible. Not that anything the Bible says is unimportant: The Holy Spirit of God spoke the whole text into existence. Every part of it was inspired by him. And he still speaks through all of it as we read the Scripture and hear it proclaimed.

But often a statement will stand out because it succinctly catches one of Scripture's great themes. Hosea 11:9 is one such verse, and particularly these words: "For I am God and not man, the Holy One in your midst. . . ." The context says that God is different from man because he is able to forgive when he should destroy. But the point holds in many contexts: God is different from us.

Not to recognize that difference is folly. To deal with that kind of foolishness, James chose two illustrations: (1) it was presumptuous for Christians to criticize their fellows; (2) it was presumptuous for the wealthy to predict their future. In both cases, territory that belonged to God was being transgressed by people.

This has been a trait of ours from the beginning of our history. We mistook the difference between God and ourselves and arrogantly assumed that we could be like God. Though our first parents were driven from the garden for trying to be like God, their progeny have been imitating their mistake ever since.

Wisdom to avoid such presumptuousness is what God wants us to have. Through James, his servant, he brought this wisdom to Christians living in the Greco-Roman world. He used two propositions to drive his wise instruction home: (1) judging a brother questions the law of Christ; (2) predicting the future challenges the will of God. These were not merely theoretical suggestions. They were comments on problems that have plagued the people of God through the centuries. We do well to look in detail at what James has said.

Judging a Brother Questions the Law of Christ

"Do not speak evil against one another, brethren. He that speaks evil against a brother or judges his brother, speaks evil against the law and judges the law. But if you judge the law, you are not a doer of the law but a judge. There is one lawgiver and judge, he who is able to save and to destroy. But who are you that you judge your neighbor?" (James 4:11–12).

Our relationship as Christians was one point that James commented on. Three times in those two verses he called Christians *brothers,* and once he called them *neighbors.* In other words, they were like a family. *Philadelphia* was one word the New Testament used to describe our relationship: the kind of love that members of a family have for each other. Care, concern, honesty, and openness—these were the qualities that brotherhood and sisterhood implied.

Note that "speaking evil" was not listed among them. Tyndale, the first great English translator of the Bible, used "backbiting" as his rendering of the word. Face-to-face rebuke was necessary at times. Christians do make mistakes. James himself had spent several chapters pointing out the mistakes of his friends. But he did it to their faces, and he did it for their good. Backbiting fails at both these points and its results are always damaging.

Christ's authority as lawgiver was the second reality James pointed to: "He that speaks evil against a brother or judges his brother, speaks evil against the law and judges the law" (4:11). What law? is our immediate question. The best answer is the law that James mentioned frequently in his letter: "the perfect law, the law of liberty" (1:25), "the royal law, according to the scripture, 'you shall love your neighbor as yourself' " (2:8). It was this law that Jesus laid down as part of the summary of all that God required of his people: "And he said to him, 'You shall love the Lord your God with all your heart, and with all your soul, and with all your mind. This is the great and first commandment. And a second is like it, You shall love your neighbor as yourself' " (Matt. 22:37–39).

Backbiting could not be squared with that law. It was by no means a neighborly gesture. God had made that clear in the book of Leviticus: "You shall not go about spreading slander among your father's kin, nor take sides against your neighbor on a capital charge. I am the Lord" (19:16, NEB). And Jesus had spoken plainly on such matters: "Judge not, that you be not judged. For with the judgment you pronounce you will be judged, and the measure you give will be the measure you get" (Matt. 7:1–2).

What were the backbiters doing? In effect they were calling Christ's law bad. They thought it so bad that they felt no obligation to obey. They flew in the face of their Lord's authority, so great was their presumptuousness.

God's authority as judge was the third aspect of the matter that James commented on. "But if you judge the law, you are not a doer of the law but a judge. There is one lawgiver and judge, he who is able to save and to destroy" (4:11–12). Theirs was the height of presumptuousness, the pinnacle of arrogance. They had taken it upon themselves to decide which of God's laws to keep and which to break. In sum, they were acting as though they were wiser than God, the only true Judge. What folly! James exclaimed. Dare you risk the consequences of questioning the authority, indeed, of usurping the authority of the heavenly Judge who holds life and death in his hands?

What may first have been excused as simple gossip had become a capital crime. It had ruptured Christian fellowship; it had defied Christ's authority; it had disputed God's sole right to judge. God is God, and we are not. "Lord, give us wisdom to cope with our presumptuousness" should be our constant prayer.

Predicting the Future Challenges the Will of God

James's second illustration of human insolence was drawn from the lives of wealthy merchants. To make his point dramatically, he addressed them as though they were present: "Come now, you who say, 'Today or tomorrow we will go into such and such a town and spend a year there and trade and get gain';

whereas you do not know about tomorrow" (4:13–14).

Phrase after phrase of arrogance was piled up in the statements of the traveling traders. The arrogance was made all the more vivid by the fact that travel in the ancient world was both dangerous and arduous. Over land one walked, or rode an animal or wagon. Roads were poor, especially where the Romans had not improved them, and robberies were frequent. At sea the ships were small, the techniques of navigation were crude, and the pirates were ready.

Almost anything could go wrong. Yet, here were merchant traders boasting of their plans and overwhelming the Christians, who had no wealth to travel, by the glowing descriptions of their itineraries.

And how confident they were! They set the times of their departures—"today or tomorrow"; they assumed that no contingencies would stop them—"we will go"; they pinpointed their destinations—"into such and such a town"; they predicted the length of their stays—"and spend a year there"; they indicated what they would be doing—"and trade"; they were sure of profitable outcomes—"and get gain."

Using their arrogance as a lesson in folly, James taught his hearers the wisdom to avoid presumptuousness. Predicting the future, James warned, challenges the will of God. Such presumptuousness is dangerous for several reasons.

We do not know enough. "You do not know about tomorrow," James chided the wealthy. They had projected themselves far into an optimistic future. They did not know enough to do that. Only God had enough foresight to know what would happen to them, and he was not saying. Wishful thinking, happy plans, and true knowledge are not the same thing. A little humility, or a lot of humility, would not hurt us at all in such circumstances.

We are not strong enough to make sure predictions about our futures. "What is your life?" James asked. "For you are a mist that appears for a little time and then vanishes" (4:14). That is language we need to hear but do not like. We use all kinds of descriptions of ourselves: successful business man; skilled professional; distinguished pastor; diligent housewife; efficient secretary; big man on campus. There is a sense in which those descriptions may be true, but we would do well to see ourselves as vanishing mists, especially if we refuse to do God's will.

James's words were undoubtedly an encouragement to his audience as well as a rebuke to the wealthy. Throughout the letter we have noted how difficult it was for Christians to relate to the wealthy. Christians seemed to have been envious, intimidated, and over-solicitous. To hear the wealthy censured for lack of knowledge and lack of strength helped them realize what true wealth was—a relationship with God, not the acquisition of money.

We must depend on God's will was the corrective that James prescribed for presumptuousness: "If the Lord wills, we shall live and we shall do this or that" (4:15). This was not to be a mechanical formula or a magical spell. It was the clear and consistent affirmation that

God was in charge. The comings and the goings, the successes and the failures of life are in his hand.

We must dismiss all arrogance: "As it is, you boast in your arrogance. All such boasting is evil" (4:16). No statement could be more pointed than that. To trust in the will of God is the only sensible attitude for the Christian to take.

If we lay our own plans and do not subject them to his will we lose on several counts: we are limited to our own wisdom; we may miss what he wants us to do; if we succeed, we may take the credit; if we fail, we face disappointment. All of these results are bad. Not trusting God for our future means losing even if we think we are winning.

We are human beings, and he is God. The difference is so vast that competition is nonsense.

The better part of wisdom is to hear his words and rejoice: "For I am God and not man." Our answer is simple: "Thank you, Lord, for being what you are; help me to remember what I am."

Neither the judge's verdict nor the prophet's foresight are skills that belong to us. Humility before the lordship of Christ and the sovereignty of God is the better part of wisdom.

"Whoever knows what is right to do and fails to do it, for him it is sin" (4:17). With those words James put us on notice. He has told us that backbiting of our neighbor and stargazing into our future are both wrong. We can never be comfortable again with presumptuousness.

11.

Wisdom to Handle Wealth

James 5:1-6

Come now, you rich, weep and howl for the miseries that are coming upon you. Your riches have rotted and your garments are moth-eaten. Your gold and silver have rusted, and their rust will be evidence against you and will eat your flesh like fire. You have laid up treasure for the last days. Behold, the wages of the laborers who mowed your fields, which you kept back by fraud, cry out; and the cries of the harvesters have reached the ears of the Lord of hosts. You have lived on the earth in luxury and in pleasure; you have fattened your hearts in a day of slaughter. You have condemned, you have killed the righteous man; he does not resist you.

The story is well known, but I need to use it to make my point. Two men, obviously down and out, were lounging against the wall of a building along Main Street. Along came a funeral procession of mam-

moth proportions. Through the windows of the luxuri-
ous hearse, they spied the gleaming silver handles
on the polished walnut casket. A black car followed
behind, loaded to its roof with elegant floral sprays.
Then came the stretched-out limousines with the im-
peccably dressed members of the family, each seated
in accordance with his or her branch of the family
tree. Then, as far as the eye could see, a line of ex-
pensive cars—many of them European—carefully
scrubbed and groomed for the occasion, carried the
hosts of mourners. The two spectators stared silently
at the dazzling array of opulence on display for the
dead man. Then one of them could contain his aston-
ishment no longer. He slapped his buddy on the shoulder as the funeral procession wheeled out of sight
and exclaimed, "Man, that's living!"

Wealth has a way of distorting our perspectives just
like that, especially if we are poor. We assume that
wealth is to be desired as one of life's finest posses-
sions and that the wealthy are the most admirable
of all creatures. Even their funerals make for fine
living.

Certainly, to Christians struggling for survival in
oppressive and impoverished circumstances, the lot
of the wealthy must have seemed attractive. The believers to whom James wrote were in grave danger
of violating Christ's law of neighbor love by their
catering to the wealthy who visited their meeting
places. Somehow they were deceived into thinking
that the wealthy as a class were better people, deserv-
ing of special honor.

James was well aware of the harm that could be done to both rich and poor by such discrimination. The wealthy could be made even more proud and self-sufficient by the adulation of the poor, and the poor would be damaged both by covetousness and by loss of self-esteem. Worse still, when the meaning and value of wealth were not held in perspective, the sense of gratitude toward God and dependence on him was dulled.

To combat this danger, James used a technique frequently employed by the Hebrew prophets. He directed a message to his own congregations by addressing an audience that was not present—the wealthy unbelievers. With strong phrases he rebuked the wealthy, not for their wealth, but for the way in which they had gained it and were handling it. An affluent society like ours in North America would do well to eavesdrop on James's sermon. No substantial group of Christians in all of history has enjoyed the financial power and the economic security that we know. There are wealthy Christians among us in large numbers, and there are many believers who are discouraged by their state of poverty. Both groups can gain from James' insights.

Wealth Is To Be Used, Not Hoarded

"Come now, you rich, weep and howl for the miseries that are coming upon you" (5:1). James's approach was startlingly dramatic. Not only did he address persons who were not present, but he also predicted a fate for them that was unexpected. Weeping and howling because of pending misery was not usually thought to be the disposition of the rich. This was shock treatment to shake the Christians out of their misunderstanding: the wicked wealthy were to be pitied, not envied, because of the fate that awaited them.

"Your riches have rotted and your garments are moth-eaten. Your gold and silver have rusted, and their rust will be evidence against you and will eat your flesh like fire. You have laid up treasure for the last days" (5:2–3). Here the problem seemed to be that of hoarding. In their attempts to pile up wealth and hold it as security for the future, the wealthy had wasted God's good gifts. Barns of grain and vats of olive oil could not be preserved indefinitely. Spoilage ("your riches have rotted") would ruin them in due season. Gold and silver became tarnished by the passing of time. While they hung unused in spacious closets, garments which were a means of both treasuring and displaying wealth fell prey to moths.

All that Jesus had warned against had come true: "Do not lay up for yourselves treasures on earth, where moth and rust consume and where thieves break in and steal, but lay up for yourselves treasure in heaven, where neither moth nor rust consumes and where thieves do not break in and steal. For where your treasure is, there will your heart be also" (Matt. 6:19–21).

Their selfishness in hoarding wealth rather than using it would backfire. They would lose what they had tried to conserve. Rot, rust, and moths would steal it from them. But that was just the beginning of their troubles. In a graphic figure of speech, James pictured the rust not only attacking the hoarded metals but eating the flesh of the hoarders. One scholar has compared the damage James describes to the damage that a corroded chain would do to the flesh it bound. The judgment of God would see to it that selfishness is duly rewarded. The real treasures waiting for them were treasures of judgment in "the last days." They had been hoarding for a rainy day or for old age. "The time will come when we need all this," they had been saying. James set them straight. "You are wrong; the time is coming when you will have to give account to God for your selfishness, and your treasure troves will be exhibit A in evidence against you." Our wealth is to be used, not hoarded.

Wealth Belongs to the Poor As Well As to the Rich

"Behold, the wages of the laborers who mowed your fields, which you kept back by fraud, cry out; and the cries of the harvesters have reached the ears of the Lord of hosts" (5:4). James was speaking to people in an agricultural society. Wealth in the form of crops, like all wealth, was the product of a great many hands. The preparation of the soil, the sowing of the seed, the weeding and cultivating, the harvesting and threshing, the grinding and milling were all tasks that required huge amounts of manual labor. Without it there would be no wealth. Yet it was the land-owners and the influential merchants who enjoyed the fruit of that labor. The slaves or peasant farmers who did the actual work lived in miserable conditions while the lords of the land wallowed in opulence.

That was not fair. Centuries before, at the beginnings of Israel's history, God had outlawed such exploitation: "You shall not oppress a hired servant who is poor and needy, whether he is one of your brethren or one of the sojourners who are in your land within your towns; you shall give him his hire on the day he earns it, before the sun goes down (for he is poor, and sets his heart upon it); lest he cry against you to the Lord, and it be sin in you" (Deut. 24:14–15).

A friend of mine in the furniture business traces a transformation in his life to the time when he began to study what the Bible had to say about the treatment of workers. This happened in the heart of the great depression when wages were low, and work was unsteady. Factory laborers would work a few days, then be laid off for days at a time, never sure what income they could count on. My friend faced a simple fact: "If the Bible is right, the employment practices in the furniture industry are wrong." From that moment on, he sought to make conditions in his factory more stable and more humane. And the Lord blessed his efforts. Now employees participate regularly in much of the company's decision-making and share in the company's profits.

Exploitation that refuses to share wealth with those who helped produce it will boomerang. Poor morale and bad workmanship are just two results that exploiters can count on. The worst result is that God knows what they are doing. His ears are open to the cries of those who are being mistreated, just as they were open to his people enslaved in Egypt. Here is his own dire promise: "Then I will draw near to you for judgment; I will be a swift witness against . . . those who oppress the hireling in his wages" (Mal. 3:5).

Who of us wants to take chances in that kind of judgment with that kind of witness? Our wealth belongs to the poor as well as to the rich.

Wealth Is to Be Used Wisely, Not Extravagantly

"You have lived on the earth in luxury and in pleasure; you have fattened your hearts in a day of slaughter" (5:5). Extravagant living had become their style. The word "pleasure" could be even stronger—"wantonness" or "wicked self-indulgence." They lived in the wild luxury that Amos had decried (6:4–6):

> Woe to those who lie on beds of ivory,
>   and stretch themselves upon their couches,
> and eat lambs from the flock,
>   and calves from the midst of the stall;
> who sing idle songs to the sound of the harp,
>   and like David invent for themselves
>   instruments of music;
> who drink wine in bowls,
>   and anoint themselves with the finest oils,
>   but are not grieved over the ruin of Joseph!

Luxury without conscience, indulgent selfishness without spiritual or moral concerns—that is a passport to judgment.

Putting personal enjoyment before concern for others brings its own backlash. James's figure of speech was harsh but telling: by their luxury the wealthy were fattening themselves like cattle to be slaughtered. That was a fierce picture of judgment. It should sober us as we consider how we are using the vast national and personal resources God has given us. Ours is one of the few societies in history where dying from overweight is a greater threat to many than dying from malnutrition. Even that may be a form of divine judgment on our excesses. Our wealth is to be used wisely, not extravagantly.

Wealth Is to Be Used Constructively, Not Abusively

"You have condemned, you have killed the righteous man; he does not resist you" (James 5:6). This was James's strongest indictment of the rich merchants. Their wealth and power were sometimes used abusively, especially in matters of law. Let a poorer man not be able to pay a debt or a widow become delinquent on her mortgage, and the creditors would haul them into court to exact full measure. Inability to pay what was owed often meant physical punishment or imprisonment. Those who had were abusing those who did not have—and taking away what little they did have, on pain of death.

Such abuse of wealth carried its own judgment. Volumes were spoken in the clause "he does not resist you." The lack of resistance made the abuse of power all the more blatant. It showed the rich man up for the bully he was. Think of the kind of judgment that Jesus' refusal to defend himself heaped on Pilate. The persecuted Christians followed their Master's example, and by their silence contributed to their oppressors' sense of guilt.

Wealth can do so much that is constructive. It is given us by God so that we can serve his causes of spreading the gospel, sustaining life, meeting needs, and providing enjoyment. It is one of the great evidences of human sin that we take goods designed to help the human family and use them in ways that hurt and oppress the very persons that most need help. Our wealth is to be used constructively, not abusively.

How we apply the lessons that we have learned looking over James's shoulder is not easy. Each of us lives in different circumstances; each of us has special needs and special obligations as we use our goods.

But some things we can say. (1) Unless we know and worship the God who gave us what we have, we are in danger of using our wealth badly. (2) No envy of the wealthy is right. They have enough problems without our making them feel more important than they really are. (3) How we use what we have is of utmost importance to God. He gave it to us, and he had his purposes, not our welfare, in mind as he did. Can we look to him for help in all this? He who bestowed wealth on our race would like also to bestow the wisdom to handle it.

"Man, that's living!" was a poor man's estimate of a posh funeral. He was wrong. It is not wealth that makes for good living, but wisdom—wisdom to use it fruitfully or wisdom to do without it contentedly.

12.

Wisdom to Wait for Christ's Coming

James 5:7-12

Be patient, therefore, brethren, until the coming of the Lord. Behold, the farmer waits for the precious fruit of the earth, being patient over it until it receives the early and the late rain. You also be patient. Establish your hearts, for the coming of the Lord is at hand. Do not grumble, brethren, against one another, that you may not be judged; behold, the Judge is standing at the doors. As an example of suffering and patience, brethren, take the prophets who spoke in the name of the Lord. Behold, we call those happy who were steadfast. You have heard of the steadfastness of Job, and you have seen the purpose of the Lord, how the Lord is compassionate and merciful.

But above all, my brethren, do not swear, either by heaven or by earth or with any other oath, but let your yes be yes and your no be no, that you may not fall under condemnation.

"A watched pot never boils." Long ago from our mothers or grandmothers we learned the truth of that old saying. We heard it when we stood by the door and waited for our father to come, edgy with impatience to tell him the day's good news. We heard it when we wondered why the bread dough took so long to rise, as our mouths watered for the hot homemade rolls. We heard it when we made twice daily treks to the garden to see whether the newly planted seeds had blossomed into the bright pictures we had admired on the packets.

"A watched pot never boils." That was a proverbial way of teaching us patience. Waiting gracefully for things we want to happen takes considerable maturity. And the maxim about the pot was a contribution our elders felt obligated to make to our maturation.

We needed it. Patience is a virtue to be prized. As we grow older and see how anxiety can corrode the disposition, if not the stomach, of those who practice it, we gain more than a passing appreciation for the lessons of patience.

Christians have always had trouble being patient. Our very faith has created the problem for us. We believe that *life ought to be different;* we are impatient with the toll that unrighteousness takes on our world; we long for the day when God will make straight all of history's crooked paths. We believe that *life will be different.* Christ's second coming is for us a fact. He has promised to return, and God has backed that promise by raising Jesus from the dead.

The brightness of that hope makes it difficult for Christ's people to be patient. History's greatest eras lie ahead, and we yearn to see that drama unfold. Especially do we yearn when we find ourselves in harsh circumstances. The newly baptized believers whom James shepherded knew that harshness and that yearning.

The unrighteousness of wealthy land owners had led to the suffering of their peasants and slaves whose underpaid task was to care for the crops. James ended the first paragraph of chapter five with this indictment: "You have condemned, you have killed the righteous man; he does not resist you" (5:6). That word, like the whole paragraph, was addressed to the wicked wealthy.

Almost before that message had time to sink in, James turned back to his fellow Christians whom he called "brethren" to show their special relationship to him in Christ, a relationship which the rich exploiters in no way shared: "Be patient, therefore, brethren, until the coming of the Lord" (5:7). An important word to spot is *therefore.* It serves as a link between the paragraphs. What James said to the Christian brethren was directly connected to what he had announced to the wealthy. One theme summarized that earlier paragraph: *judgment.* God would see to it that the wicked would be paid full measure for their selfishness. The believers' task was, therefore, a simple one: they were to wait for Christ's appearing. And they were given specific instructions about what to do and what not to do while they waited.

What to Do While We Wait

"*Be patient,* therefore, brethren, until the coming of the Lord. Behold, the farmer waits for the precious fruit of the earth, being patient over it until it receives the early and the late rain. You also be patient . . ." (5:7–8, emphasis added).

Patience, or long-suffering, as the word could be translated, is not easy to cultivate. But James pointed out that there are certain walks of life where patience must be the rule. Farming was and is one of those. Drought presses the long-suffering of farmers beyond recognition. Their land is ready; their trees are waiting; their field hands are standing by. The whole agricultural enterprise with its hybrid seeds, its grafted trees, its automated sprinklers, its chemical fertilizers is waiting for one thing—rain. Farmers, even in more favorable weather conditions, have only two choices: to learn patience or to quit farming. They are totally dependent on the water supply—"the early and the late rain," James called it. In Palestine rain in October was necessary to prepare the soil, and rain in March and April to bring the harvest of barley and wheat to its full maturity.

The farming illustration points not only to the *need for patience*—rain comes only when it is ready; it also points to the *rewards of patience*—the "precious fruit" is worth waiting for. With it the farmer cares for his family, pays his mortgage, gains seed for next year, and feeds a neighborhood.

James's meaning was plain: when we consider whom we are waiting for and what his coming will mean, then patience is not too high a price to pay. Our long-suffering will be amply rewarded by God's justice which will set all wrongs right.

The word *coming* itself rings with hope and glory. It is the word used to describe the visit of a king or a general to a city that will receive him with honor. It speaks of pageantry and dignity, of martial trumpets and prancing horses, of waving spectators and flower-strewn streets, of gates flung open and royalty received. Our Lord's coming is that kind of event and more. It gives us good reason to be patient while we wait.

"Establish your hearts, for the coming of the Lord is at hand" (5:8). This was the second thing James wanted his friends to do while they waited. "Be strong in your assurance and confidence; your waiting will not be in vain. In fact, it is almost over." That would be a paraphrase of James' remarks.

Establish your hearts to *keep hoping when the delay seems interminable.* Waiting is hard work. We keep wondering "When?" and "Why not now?" Doubts begin to fester in our minds. Our hope of Christ's return becomes clouded with uncertainty. What should be life's greatest exclamation point—Christ is coming!—becomes life's largest question mark—Is Christ coming? Hold fast, James has said, "for the coming of the Lord is at hand."

Establish your hearts to *keep trusting when God's timing seems questionable.* "How long?" was a favorite question of Israel's psalmists. Sufferers ever since have echoed that complaint. Think how passionately our Jewish brothers and sisters must have lifted that cry—"How long?"—in the Nazi death camps. If ever there was a time when, humanly speaking, Messiah should have come, it was then. But God did not time his intervention on their terms. We do not understand why the Father, who alone knows the hour, has delayed Christ's coming. We do not know why he allows unrighteousness, injustice, and unbelief to thrive unchecked. But we do know that no circumstances in heaven, earth, or hell have authority to countermand the edict of God. We can wait in confidence, even when our waiting is puzzling and painful, knowing that Christ's coming is at hand.

Establish your hearts to *keep working for righteousness when results seem meager.* We are waiting for Christ, not loitering. One way to ease the pain of waiting is to keep busy. That was part of what grandmother had in mind when she taught us patience from the pot that refused to boil while we watched. She was really saying, "Get on with another chore or two and the kettle will whistle much sooner."

According to God's promise, "we wait for new heavens and a new earth in which righteousness dwells" (2 Pet. 3:13). While we wait for righteousness, we also work for it. Our deeds of love, our thoughtful votes, our protests of wickedness and corruption, our holy lives, our daily prayers, our faithful witness to God's saving power—these are all deeds that work for righteousness in the midst of our fallen, wayward world. Yet success seems so slow; wickedness and unbelief seem so unyielding; hardened hearts seem so impenetrable to God's ways. James's word is timely: we are to keep working at righteousness, even when it does not seem to pay, supported by the confidence that "the coming of the Lord is at hand."

What Not to Do While We Wait

"Do not grumble, brethren, against one another, that you may not be judged; behold, the Judge is standing at the doors" (5:9). Two reminders stood out in this verse, as James instructed his hearers in what not to do while they waited. They were not to let their impatience strain their relationships with each other. Waiting has a way of doing that. A night spent with fog-bound passengers in an airport is all the evidence we need. Tempers are short; complaints are frequent. People blame others for circumstances over which they have no control. Christ's church must do better than that. Groaning over our frustrations and anxieties should not crowd love, praise, and graciousness out of our daily living, even in stretching circumstances.

James' other reminder was very direct: Christians are accountable to God just as unbelievers are. Unrighteousness in the church is no prettier than unrighteousness outside. The Judge who stands at the door holds us accountable even while he asks us to wait.

One of the reasons we are accountable is that we have such extraordinary examples of patience before us in the Scriptures: "As an example of suffering and patience, brethren, take the prophets who spoke in the name of the Lord. Behold, we call those happy

who were steadfast. You have heard of the steadfastness of Job, and you have seen the purpose of the
Lord, how the Lord is compassionate and merciful"
(5:10–11).

James's illustrations were good ones. Anyone who
has read the story of Jeremiah and that of Job knows
how much they suffered. They did not suffer silently.
They were human beings, not angels. Their suffering
brought them to the breaking point. But they were
good examples in two ways: (1) they brought their
complaints directly to God rather than using them
to hurt other persons; (2) they held fast to their hope
in God's rightness even when they disliked what he
was doing. This openness before God and this commitment to God gave them the happy toughness that
saw them through their difficulties. They did not always know God's purposes. Neither do we. But they
always knew that behind the mystery of ways that
seemed harsh there stood a Lord whose heart is merciful and compassionate. If it takes painful waiting for
us to learn such lessons, so be it!

"But above all, my brethren, *do not swear,* either
by heaven or by earth or with any other oath, but
let your yes be yes and your no be no, that you may
not fall under condemnation" (5:12). No grumbling
against others; love is to be the law while we wait.
Then James took the lesson one step further. No
swearing against God; fear of his name must mark
our attitudes, even when the going is rough.

Pain can make us rash and irreverent. It breaks out
the worst in us, drives ut to extremes. Blasphemy can

be the result when we use God's name lightly. We can damn others with the name of God under the pressures of our frustrations. We can defame God by using parts of his creation—like heaven or earth—to swear by, as though they somehow shared his sacredness.

Christian discipleship—even painful discipleship—has no right to any such irreverence. Simple, direct, trustworthy speech—where yes means yes and no means no—is our best safeguard. "Hallowed be thy name" was what Jesus taught his first disciples as the first petition in their life of prayer. Any speech pattern that does not fit that theme is to be avoided at all cost, no matter how frustrated and anxious we are tempted to become.

If patience is a virtue while we watch for a pot to boil, how much more while we wait for a Savior to come. An appropriate prayer would be: Lord, amid shadows that loom dark with discouragement, let the light of Christ's coming flood my heart with brightness beyond telling.

13.

Wisdom to Pray Effectively

James 5:13-20

Is any one among you suffering? Let him pray. Is any cheerful? Let him sing praise. Is any among you sick? Let him call for the elders of the church, and let them pray over him, anointing him with oil in the name of the Lord; and the prayer of faith will save the sick man, and the Lord will raise him up; and if he has committed sins, he will be forgiven. Therefore confess your sins to one another, and pray for one another, that you may be healed. The prayer of a righteous man has great power in its effects. Elijah was a man of like nature with ourselves and he prayed fervently that it might not rain, and for three years and six months it did not rain on the earth. Then he prayed again and the heaven gave rain, and the earth brought forth its fruit.

My brethren, if any one among you wanders from the truth and some one brings him back, let him know that whoever brings back a sinner from the error of his way will save his soul from death and will cover a multitude of sins.

Biblical wisdom is neither shrewd nor clever. It is not a way of hoodwinking our friends or outwitting our enemies. Nor is it a matter of just doing what works. Because it is wisdom from above, it is wisdom that always has God in the picture. Consequently, it is a wisdom that works.

It may learn from good examples, but it does not take its cues from human experience alone. It may be wise in the ways of the world, but it is not based on worldly wisdom. It may have a keen sense of what human beings have found to be right and wrong, but it is not limited to human judgments.

James made that clear at the beginning of his letter when he instructed his Christian friends in where to find wisdom: "If any of you lacks wisdom, let him ask God, who gives to all men generously and without reproaching, and it will be given him" (1:5).

Here James called attention to the link between wisdom and prayer. No wisdom from above is available without the humble asking that we call prayer. Students of Socrates once asked him why he was so wise. Candidly and modestly he told them that if his wisdom outran that of his fellows, the reason was a simple one: he was aware of how little wisdom one really has, and they were not.

Socrates' words are wise ones for us to follow. We do not have enough wisdom on our own to cope with a life that is full of suffering, to guard against hostility toward our enemies and favoritism toward the wealthy, to control our vile tongues, to trust God for our future plans, to understand both the perils and the responsibilities of riches, to wait patiently for the Lord of glory to return. "Pray for wisdom" was one of James's first commands to his needy audience. He then proceeded to help answer their prayers by giving them lesson after lesson in the ways that wisdom worked.

But he could not conclude his lessons without coming back to the subject of prayer. He chose to end his words of wisdom on the theme with which he began. Praying for wisdom was the beginning note; wisdom for praying was the closing. In both, one thing was plain: wisdom means depending on God in every circumstance. The psalmist gave us a useful definition of a fool: "The fool says in his heart, 'There is no God'" (Ps. 14:1). To live as though God did not exist is the hallmark of folly. If that be true, then the essence of wisdom must be to acknowledge our total dependence on God. Is not that what the wise man meant in these words from Proverbs? "The fear of the Lord is the beginning of knowledge; fools despise wisdom and instruction" (1:7).

Prayer must play a key part in our fear of God. Through prayer we acknowledge our inability to be wise on our own; we beg God for love, patience, and understanding in a world where these are so badly needed; we thank God for the supply of wisdom that he gives; we repent to him over how poorly we use it.

Instruction in effective praying was the most practical and fitting way that James could find to close his letter. It was the climax, moreover, of the advice he had been giving about Christ's second coming. They were to have patient, confident hearts as they waited for the Messiah to return and establish his righteous rule. And their tongues were to express that confidence by not grumbling against each other or swearing rash oaths.

Instead, their tongues were to busy themselves with prayer. Four themes emerged from James's compact and powerful lesson: (1) prayer is always appropriate—no circumstance puts us out of reach of God; (2) prayer is often corporate—other members of Christ's body can share the experience with us; (3) prayer is totally subject to God's will—we must trust him for guidance in how to pray; (4) prayer is frequently an encouragement to restoration—the best way to reach the wandering believer is by praying for him or her. Wisdom to pray effectively was James's final subject. These four themes were its heart.

Prayer Is Always Appropriate

Control of the tongue had been one of James's keen concerns. The tongue was the bit that guided the horse, the rudder that steered the ship, the fire that ignited the forest. Much of what our tongue does, James considered inappropriate: "With it we bless the Lord and Father, and with it we curse men, who are made in the likeness of God" (3:9). The tongue was to be used with exceeding care by the few people genuinely called to be teachers, because theirs was an especially weighty responsibility (3:1). They had great power either to heal or to hurt by what they said. Much of what their tongues did was inappropriate.

But one use of the tongue was suited to everyone—not just the carefully chosen teachers. Everyone could pray. And everyone could pray in all circumstances. Prayer was always appropriate: "Is any one among you suffering? Let him pray. Is any cheerful? Let him sing praise" (5:13).

By pointing a finger at the contrasting experiences—suffering and cheerfulness—James was gesturing at everything in between. *We can pray in all seasons.* No emotion of ours is a secret to our heavenly Father; no feeling of ours is beyond the competence of the Comforter who dwells within us; no experience of ours is foreign to the Christ who bore our human flesh. The triune God—Father, Spirit, and Son—can cope with our circumstances no matter what plight we find ourselves in. Nothing excludes God's people from the right to pray; nothing excludes God's people from the need to pray.

We can find fit prayers to pray in all seasons. James mentioned two types: prayers of petition and praise. There are many variations of these types, as the Psalms of the Bible show us. They are a great compendium of prayer and praise for all sorts of situations. Part of God's goodness to us in the Bible is his provision of prayers for us to use. He did not leave our praying to accident. He furnished us with superb models from the life of Israel, his people. And he gave us the supreme pattern of prayer and praise in the words Jesus taught his disciples.

Prayer Is Often Corporate

James knew that there were circumstances in which personal prayer was very difficult. Illness was one of them. It sapped the strength, taxed the morale, and challenged the faith of the believers. James included a special word for them: "Is any among you sick? Let him call for the elders of the church, and let them pray over him, anointing him with oil in the name of the Lord; and the prayer of faith will save the sick man, and the Lord will raise him up; and if he has committed sins, he will be forgiven" (5:14–15).

The member of the congregation is not alone. In his days of weakness he is to remember that he belongs to a body. He can count on the stronger members to support him with their prayers. The love of those who come to pray can be used to contribute to the healing.

The elders of the congregation are on call. Their tasks are not just administration and teaching. They must be chosen for their spiritual maturity, their confidence in God, their pastoral concern.

This combination of need and response points to what the church is about. We share our weaknesses and our strengths. The spiritual resources of the stronger are put at the disposal of the weaker. Christian fellowship shows up best for what it is when the pains of one person are ministered to by the love of others. Prayer is often corporate. It is an expression of the fact that Christ has put us together for the help and service of each other.

Prayer Is Totally Subject to God's Will

James's language was confident but careful. His words were delicately chosen. He wanted to give full encouragement about the power of prayer, yet he did not want to make it magical or automatic. It was important for him to make clear that prayer is totally subject to God's will.

It is prayer, not personal power, that is to be used. No magic spell or mystical rite was mentioned. The only qualification of those called was that they were elders. It was not their personal or spiritual gifts that made the difference. They could not manipulate God.

The anointing with oil points to the work of God's Spirit. The oil of itself had no power; it was a sign of dependence on God. It harked back to the Old Testament ritual of anointing in which priests, kings, and prophets were filled with the Holy Spirit in order to render their service to God.

The name of the Lord is called upon. We bring no ability or merit to our prayers. We have access to God only through his Son Jesus. We do not muscle our way to the throne of God by our own efforts; we do not brashly present our own credentials. We plead the name of Jesus; we gain entrée to God because Jesus has become for us the way. Our prayer and our anointing has significance only because of him.

The effective prayer is the prayer of faith. The prayer prayed in faith is dependent on God's will. Faith, here, cannot mean the general belief that God *can* heal; it must mean the specific assurance that God *will* heal in this case. Such faith is God's gift, not our presumptuousness. We cannot tell God when he has to heal; we can only ask him when he wants to heal.

I remember an emergency that my friend Steve went through when he was seriously burned by roofing tar many years ago. His wife Naomi summoned me to the hospital. The doctor's words were grim— at least ten weeks of healing and then extensive skin grafting. When the doctor left the room, Naomi and I prayed. I began to ask that the Lord's will be done, yet even as I did I felt a leading from the Lord to pray for healing. At that moment the Lord gave me faith to ask for rapid recovery. Steve left the hospital after a month or so—and no skin grafting was necessary. The prayer of faith had been used to save the sick man.

Part of the Lord's healing is forgiveness. No illness should lead us to neglect the spiritual aspects of life. The leaders of a congregation that care for the ill must also be mindful of their personal relationships to God through Jesus Christ. Wholeness with him means more than physical healing; it means the peace and joy that come from his forgiveness.

It is the Lord who raises up the ill. Not the elders, not their prayers, not the oil, not the repentance of sins—none of these can heal. Only the Lord can do that. Our prayer is totally subject to God's will.

Yet we are encouraged to pray to give God an opportunity to work his will. And where we are genuinely open to do that will and to accept his ways, marvelous things happen. Elijah's prayer for drought and then rain in Ahab's day was James's illustration. We should take heart from one clause: "Elijah was a man of like nature with ourselves . . . " (5:17). Not an angel, not a superman, not a semi-god, Elijah had all the limitations that we have. Yet his prayer changed the course of human history.

Prayer Is Frequently an Encouragement to Restoration

James' final word had to do with helping the backsliders. They were the spiritually ill, who needed the help of the other believers as much as the physically ill: "My brethren, if any one among you wanders from the truth and some one brings him back, let him know that whoever brings back a sinner from the error of his way will save his soul from death and will cover a multitude of sins" (5:19–20).

At times prayer is the only means we have to encourage the wanderer to return. *Prayer does not depend on the backslider's cooperation.* We can pray for a person who will not listen to us. We can pray for a person who will not attend church with us. Prayer for the wayward is one of the great acts of love. It means praying despite disappointment, rejection, and frustration.

Praying keeps us open to reconciliation. It shields us from bitterness and vindictiveness. It is hard to stay angry at persons for whom we pray. Our very prayer may contribute to their return, especially as that loving prayer is backed by our deeds of love.

Prayer works lasting results. It may save a sinner from judgment and may also keep others from following in his course. Every backslider is the source of great potential damage in a congregation or a community. Concerted prayer to head them off from destroying themselves and others can literally "cover a multitude of sins."

Wisdom from above! It comes in many forms. All of them involve firm dependence on God, without whom all of life will turn foolish. Wisdom is variegated in its tones and colors. Like love, to which it is a close cousin, wisdom is a many-splendored thing. But nothing we do, in word or deed, shows as clearly that we have learned wisdom's high lessons as when we pray. Wisdom begins with the fear of God; the fear of God begins in prayer.

Conclusion

Guidelines for the progress of Christian pilgrims—
that is a suitable description of the contents of James's
letter. "The twelve tribes of the Dispersion" to whom
he addressed his greetings and his instructions (1:1)
were pilgrim Christians, citizens of heaven though sojourners on earth. The Apostle's purpose was plain:
to help his loved ones fulfill their heavenly calling
amidst their earthly perils.

The world, the flesh, and the devil formed the context of those perils. The problems of the Christians
in the infant churches were *social:* the political, economic, and social structure of the world both treated
them harshly and prompted them to envy or rebellion.
Their problems were also *personal:* harsh vengeance
in the face of suffering, rash impatience while waiting
for the Lord to come, sharp tongues that criticize and
backbite, cruel discrimination that caters to the rich
and starves the poor, fleshly competition that wars
for pride of station. Their problems, furthermore,
were *spiritual:* they wavered between faith and doubt;
they believed Christian doctrines and neglected Christian love; they affirmed God's wisdom and practiced
the devil's.

No wonder these pilgrims needed sharp correction from their wise teacher and pastor. *The uncompromising uniqueness of Christ's people* was one strong lesson that James taught them. There were two great ways that the human family could follow: the way of the world or the way of God. Those ways were divergent, not parallel. The way of the world was marked by selfishness, waywardness, and finally judgment. The way of the Lord was characterized by love, discipline, and, at the end, the happiness of divine approval. One could not walk both ways simultaneously. God's people, like their Master who lived among them, were to be unique—stamped with wisdom from above, wisdom that works.

James's second lesson flowed logically from his first: *the unembarrassed dependence on God's provisions.* Selfishness, doubt, foolishness, spiritual poverty—those are natural traits. We do not have to work hard to cultivate them. What was important was for God's pilgrims to confess, without fear or shame, their helplessness, their inability to handle inner struggles or outer conflicts without his help. He is the Father of lights, the Giver of every good and perfect gift, the righteous Judge, the divine Healer, the merciful Forgiver. His hand determined their lot; his will directed their course; his wisdom shaped their lives; his Word taught them true religion. Like children, wide-eyed and open-faced, their heads were to be lifted and their hands outstretched to him.

The third lesson was the inevitable outcome of the first two: *the unhesitating call to total commitment.* As

God's own people, separated from worldly values and dependent on God's grace, the scattered Christians were called to submit their lives to God's will and God's purposes. Double-mindedness, bitter speech, and contentious strife were to be banished. Life whether in the fields, the marketplace, the home, or the synagogue was to be life under God. His terms set the rules, his righteousness formed the standard. No area of their existence was exempt. The Creator who is the Redeemer was to be their Lord. No easy division into sacred and secular, commercial and spiritual, private and public was tolerable. All of life was God's terrain.

This rough summary of the problems of James's people and the solutions he offered them tells us how little has changed in 1900 years. The letter is ancient but not musty; it is durable, not obsolete. The churches of Jesus Christ are yet "the twelve tribes of Israel in the Dispersion." The Israel of God is moving toward the completion of their mission, and the Lord, the Messiah, is at hand; "the Judge is standing at the doors" (5:9). This gives us all the more incentive to make these final days of our pilgrimage count.

For us the Book of James is as contemporary as a freeway map. We can count on it not to lead us astray.

James is a *paradigm* to help us test our attitudes and activities. The love, the patience, the poise, the peaceableness that should be the traits of Christian disciples are spelled out in its pages with a clarity that cannot be missed.

James is a *catalyst* to a more thorough and practical

spirituality. Assimilating it—letting it be the "implanted word" (1:21) in our lives—will allow the chemistry of the gospel to permeate every area of our personalities and to bring its powers of wondrous transformation.

James is a *signal* that Christian doctrine is not just an intellectual game like chess; it is motivation and power for worship and service. Theology is for discipleship, this letter has reminded us. Any theology that does not lead to control of tongue and temper, to unity and harmony within the church, to prayerful wisdom and wise prayer, and to compassionate action toward the poor, the widow, and the orphan is not sound theology—no matter how high-flown its propositions, no matter how pretentious its presenters.

A paradigm for pilgrims! May we conjugate our verbs of sound thinking and right living by James's pattern?

A catalyst for Christians! Can we absorb its vitality and open ourselves to its lasting changes?

A signal for saints! Will our ears and hearts be open to its persistent practicality that summons us to be "doers of the word, and not hearers only"?